NAUTICAL NAMASTE

A Sealife Pattern Escape

TWIN FAWN MEDIA

TWIN FAWN MEDIA

Published by Twin Fawn Media
www.twinfawnmedia.com
Portland, Maine

ISBN-13 978-0997733303
ISBN-10 0997733306

Cover design by Becky Chase.

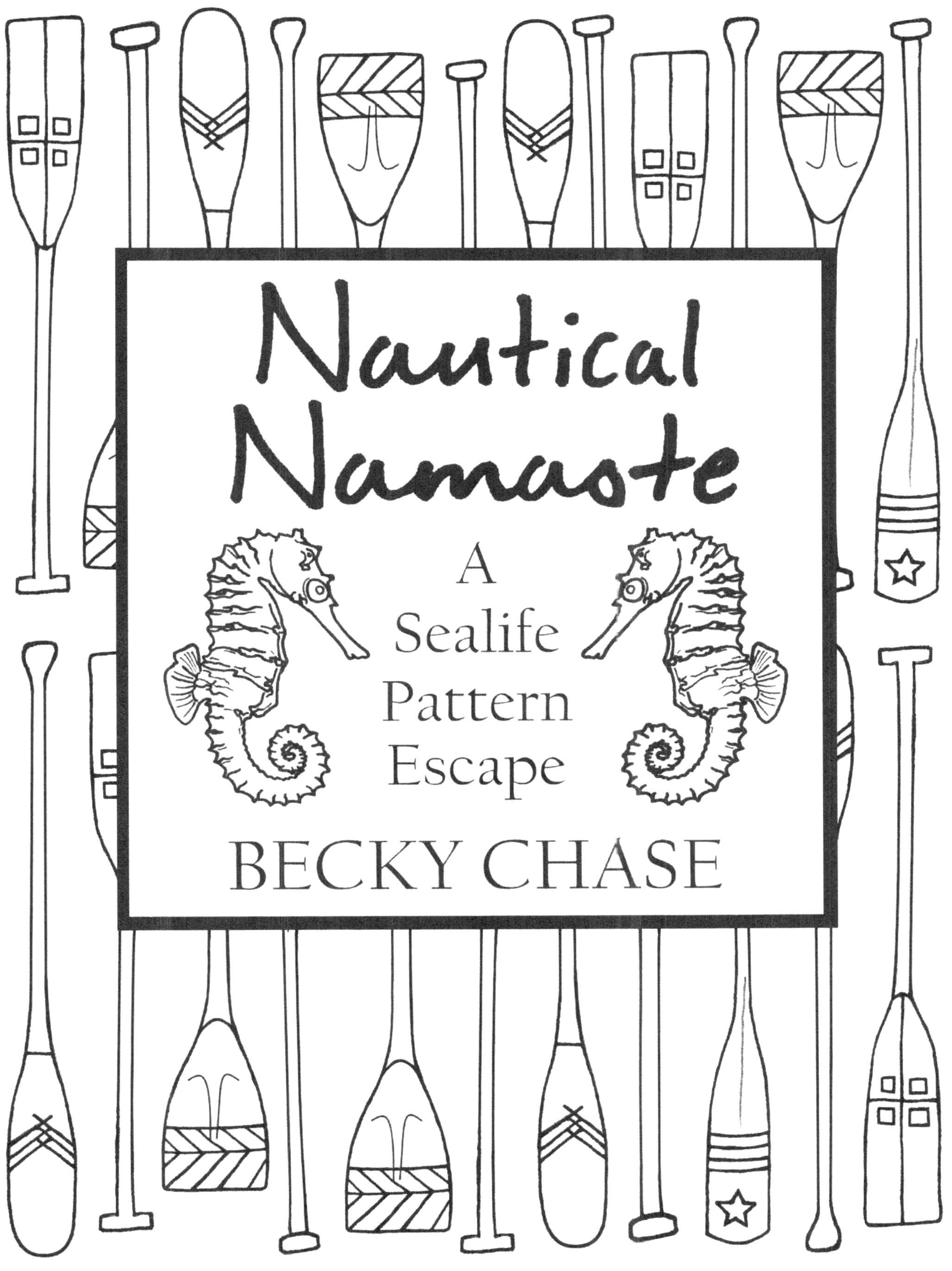

Nautical
Namaste
A
Sealife
Pattern
Escape
BECKY CHASE

In Loving Memory of

ROBERT INGALLS CHASE

1948 - 2009

"Consider the subtleness of the sea; how its most dreaded creatures glide under water, unapparent for the most part, and treacherously hidden beneath the loveliest tints of azure... Consider all this; and then turn to this green, gentle, and most docile earth; consider them both, the sea and the land; and do you not find a strange analogy to something in yourself?"

- Herman Melville, *Moby Dick; or, The Whale*

"Because there's nothing more beautiful than the way the ocean refuses to stop kissing the shoreline, no matter how many times it's sent away."

- Sarah Kay

NOTE ON COLOR APPLICATION

Crayons, colored pencils, and marker pens can all be used on the drawings in this book.

If using marker pens, it may be worthwhile to place an extra sheet of paper behind a page in case of bleed-through.

Most importantly, have fun!

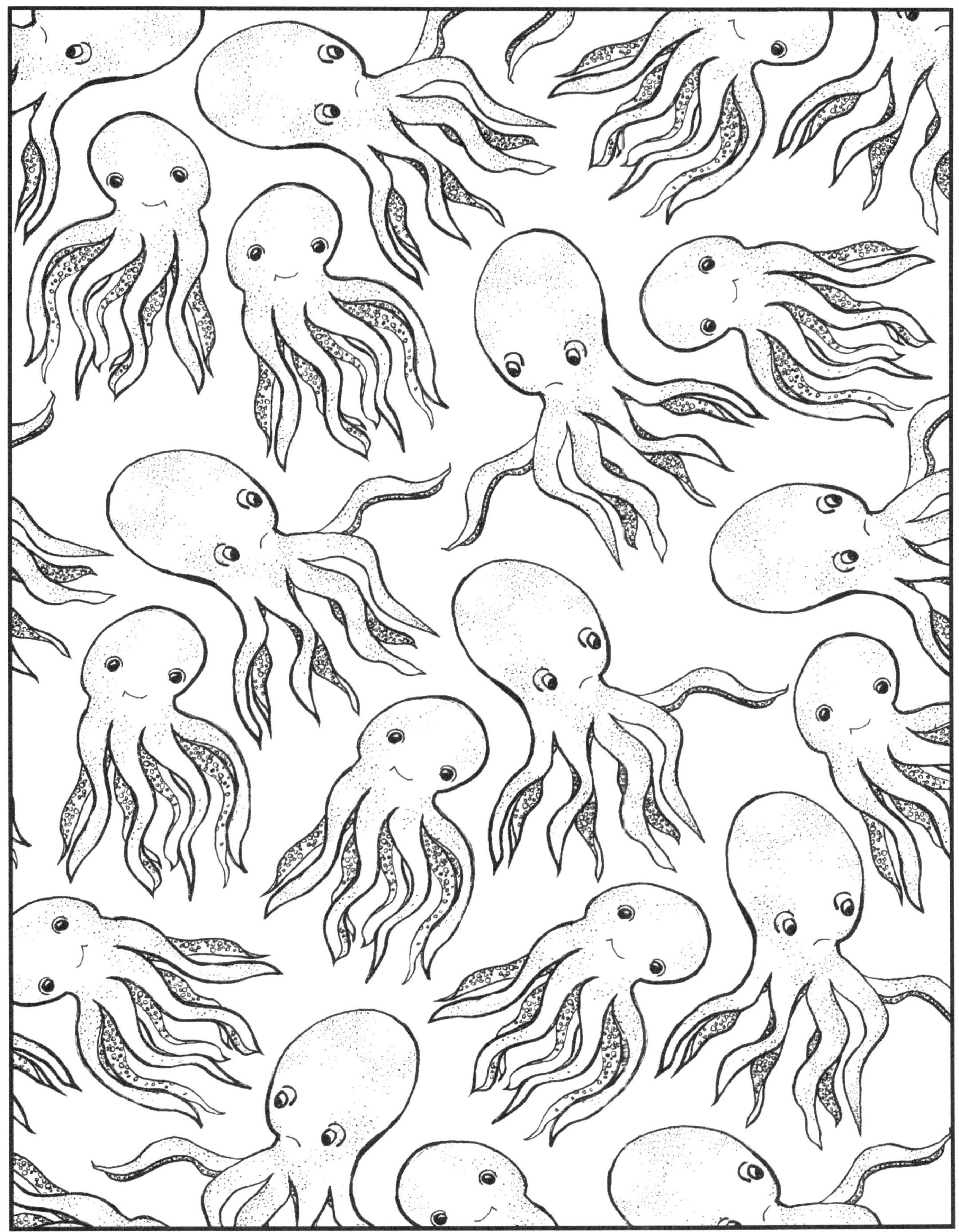

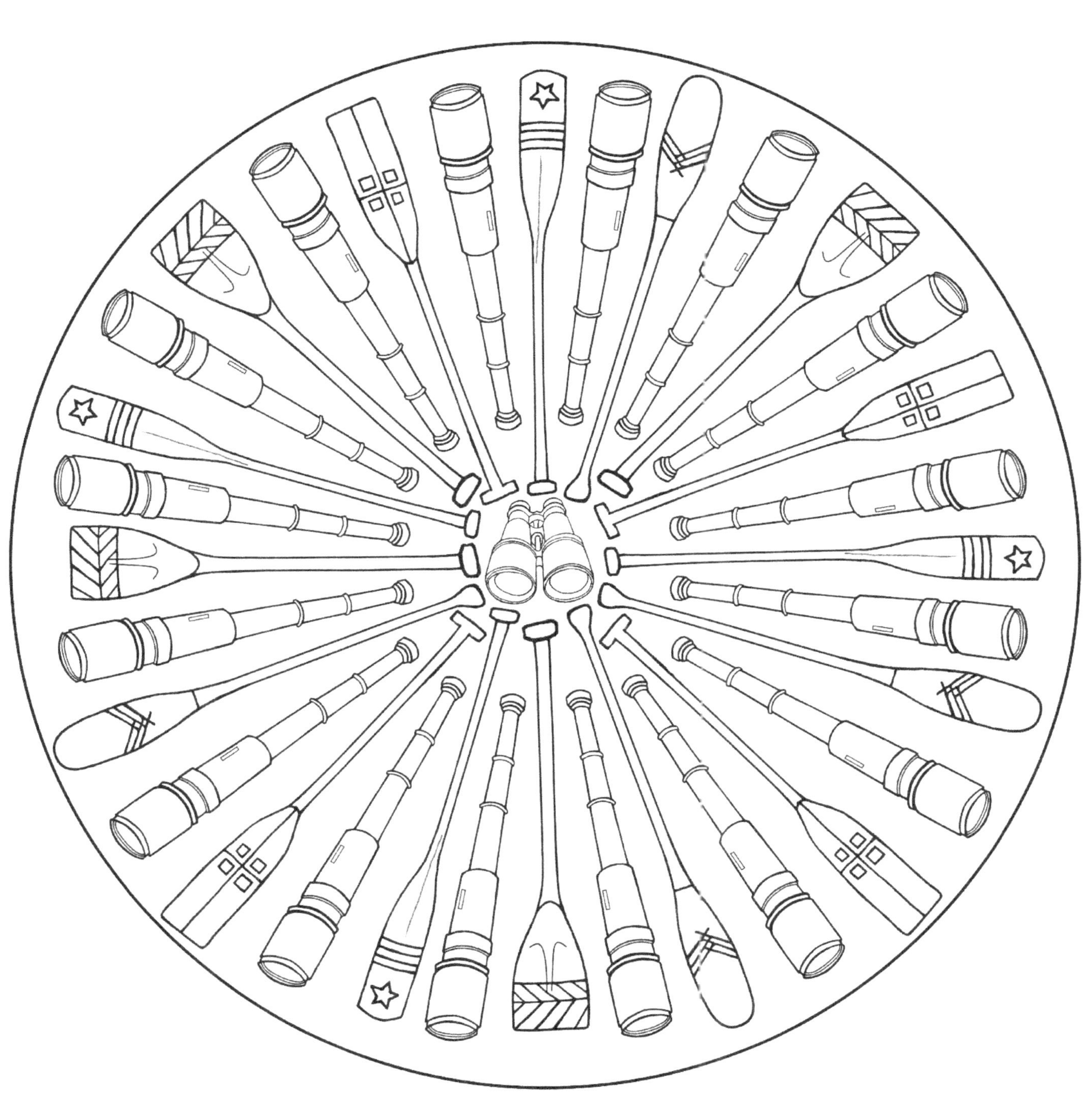

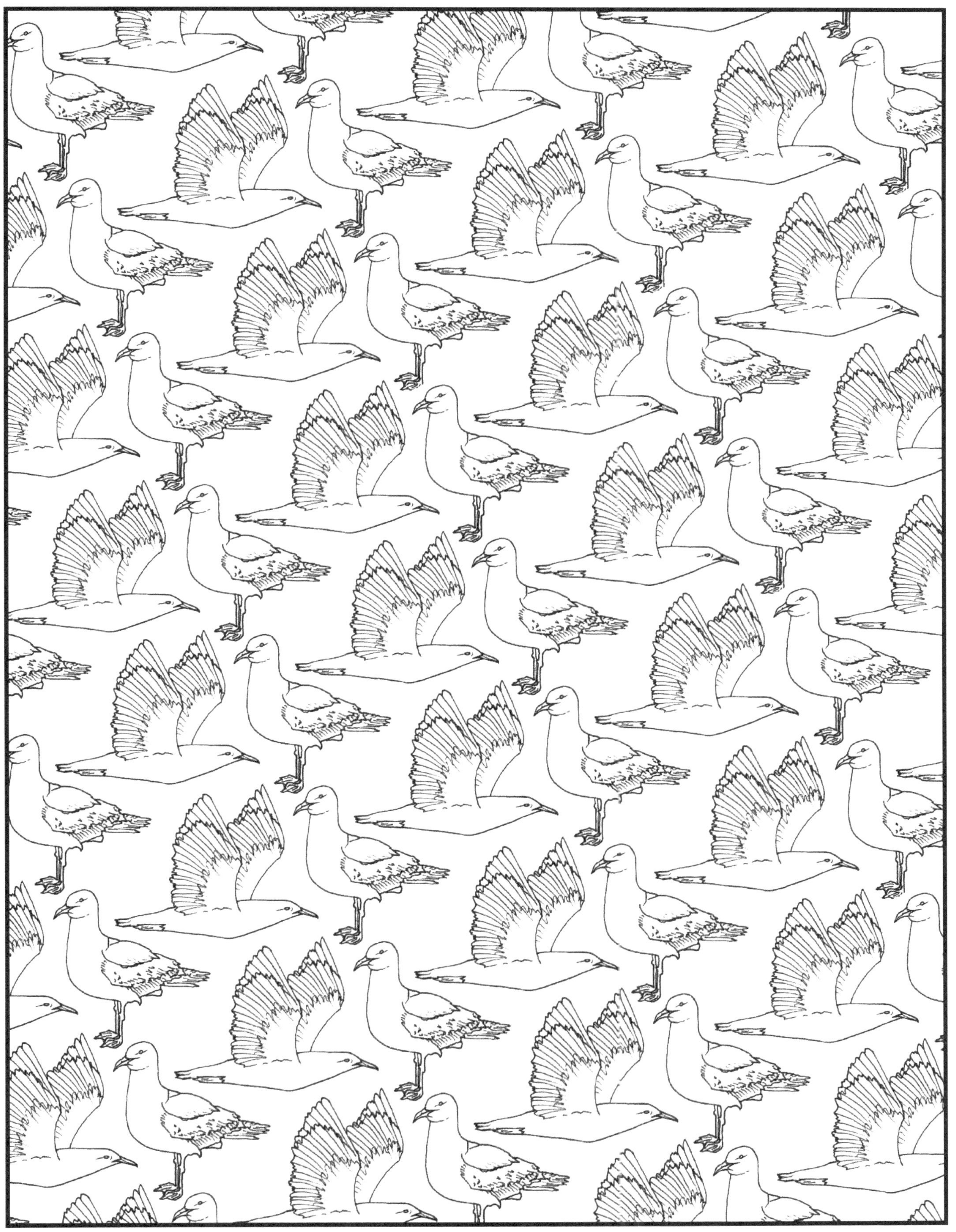

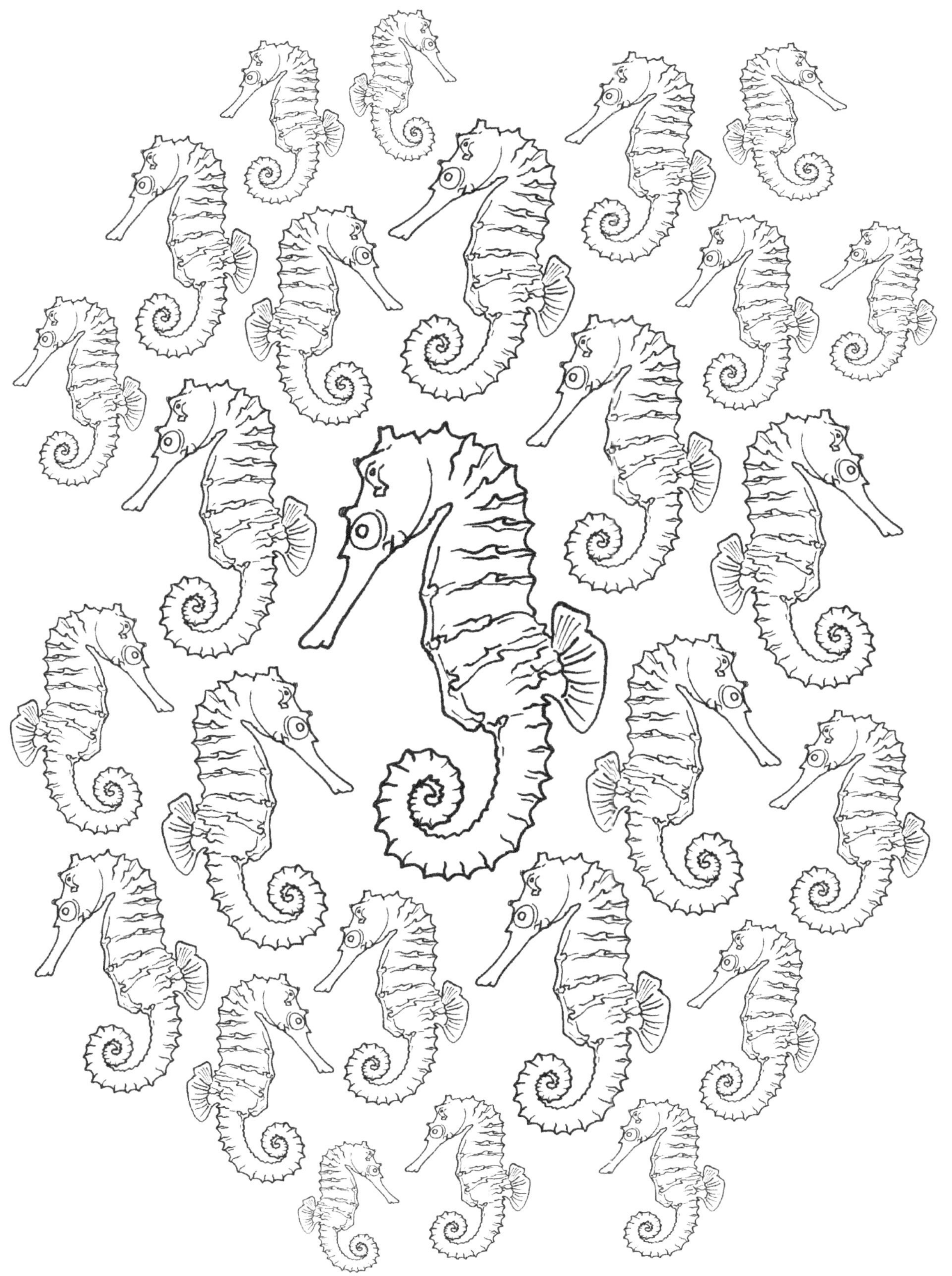

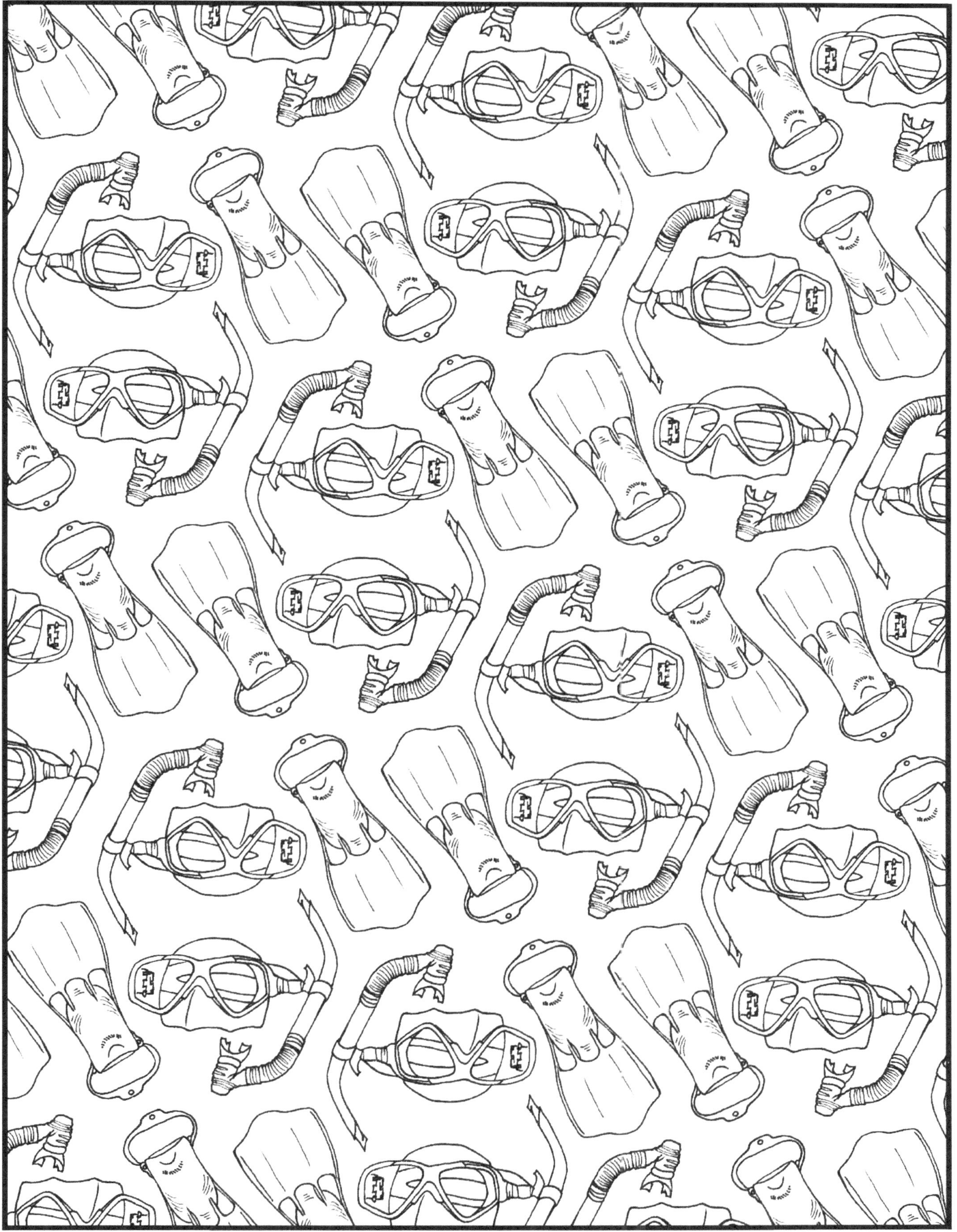

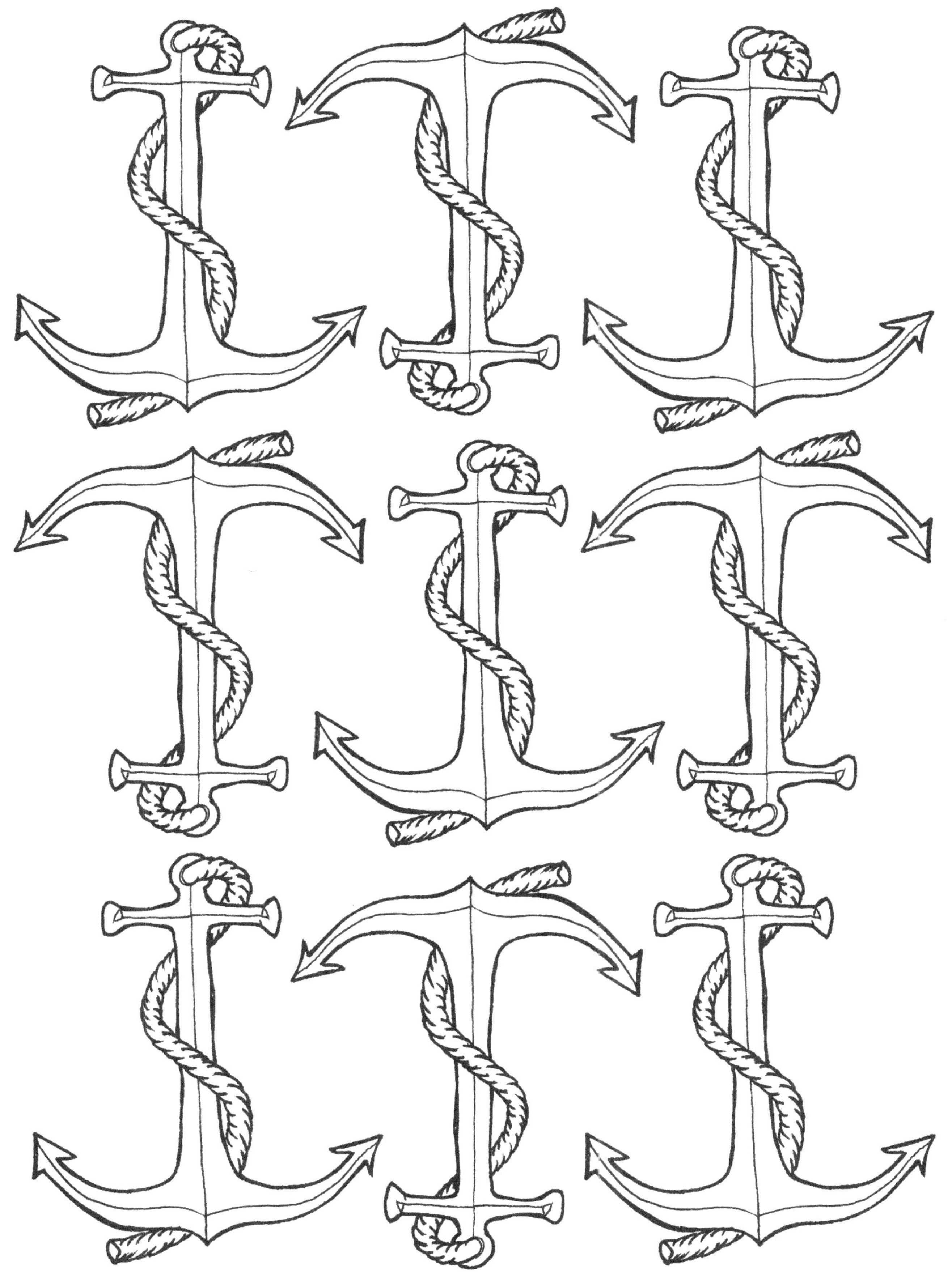

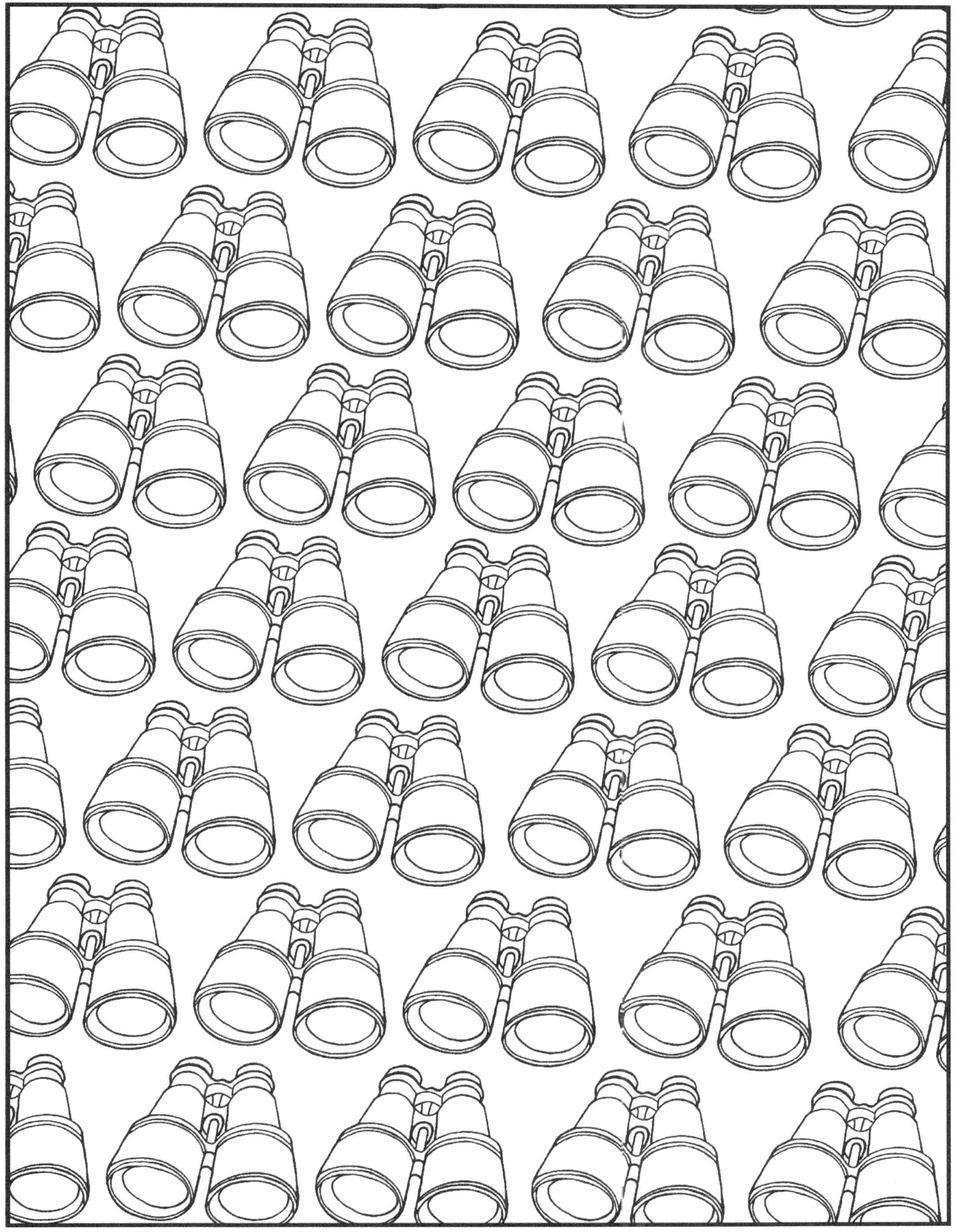

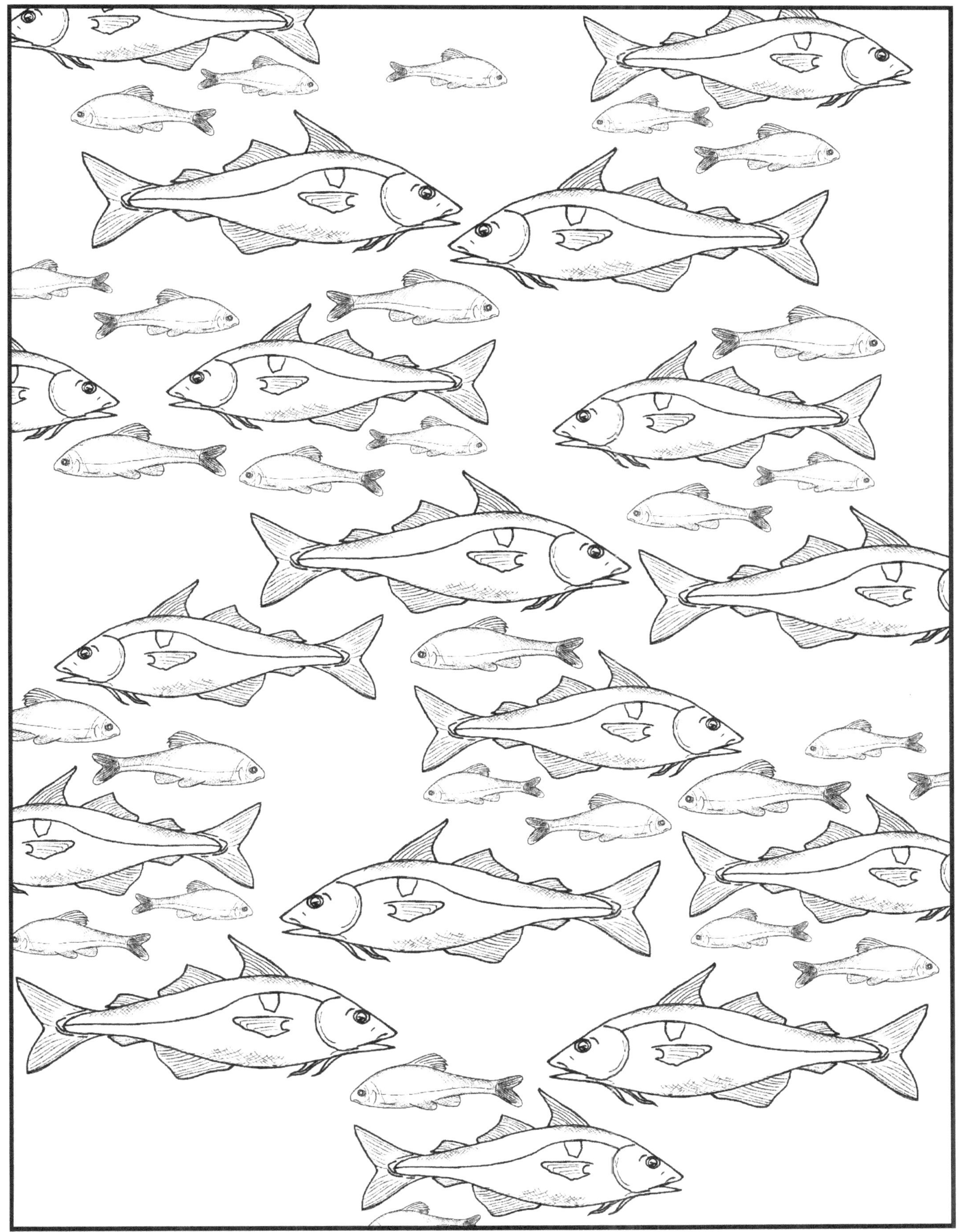

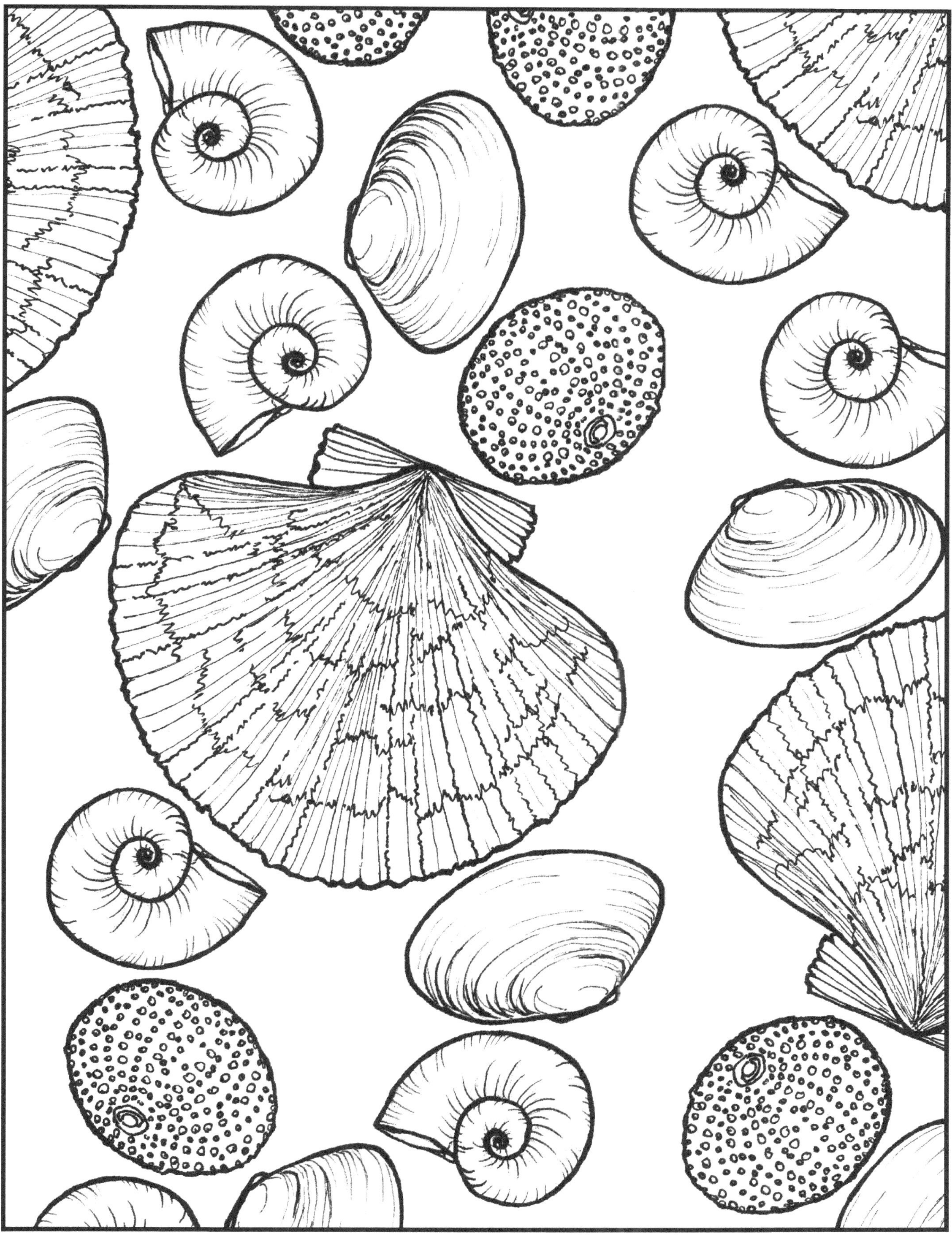

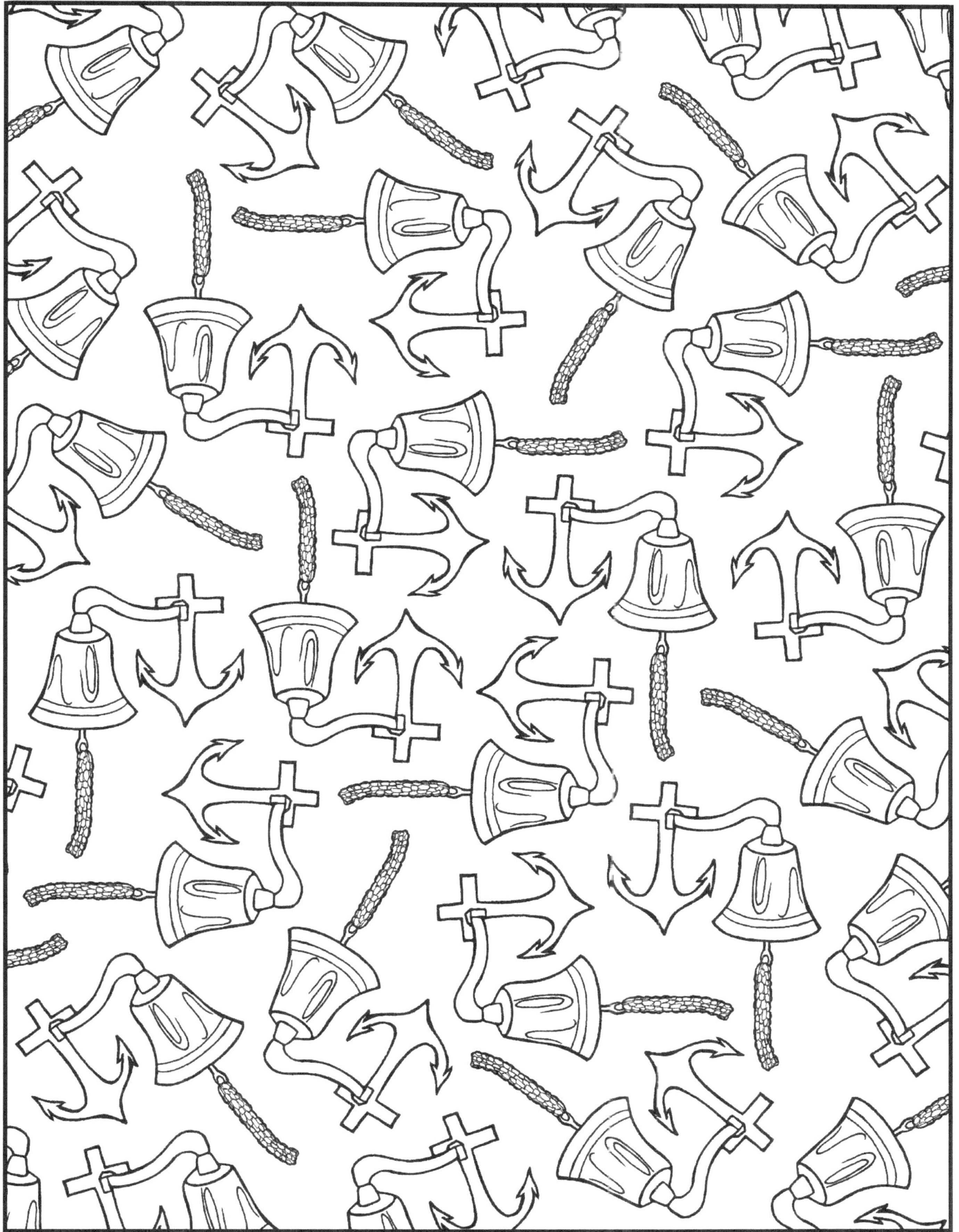

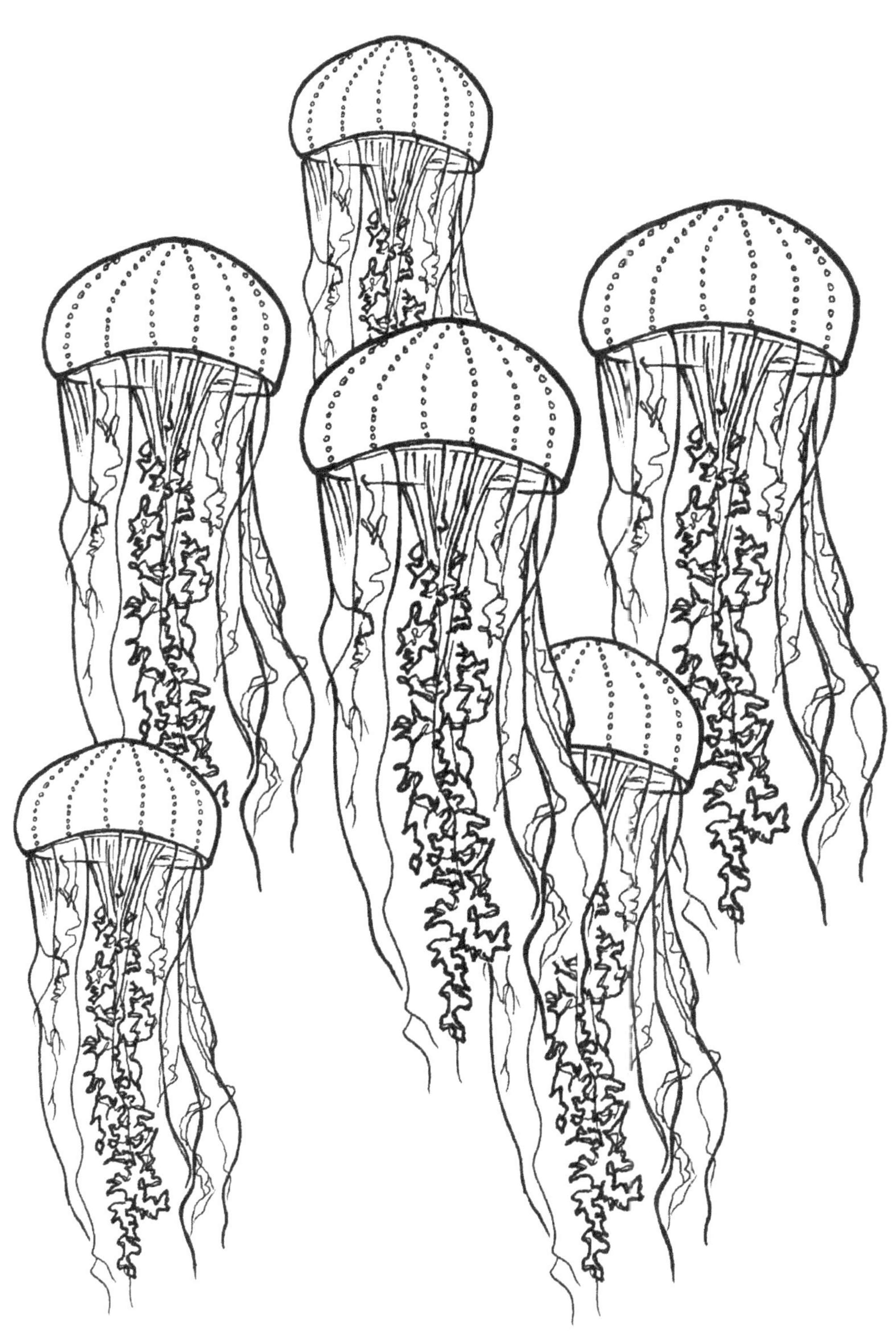

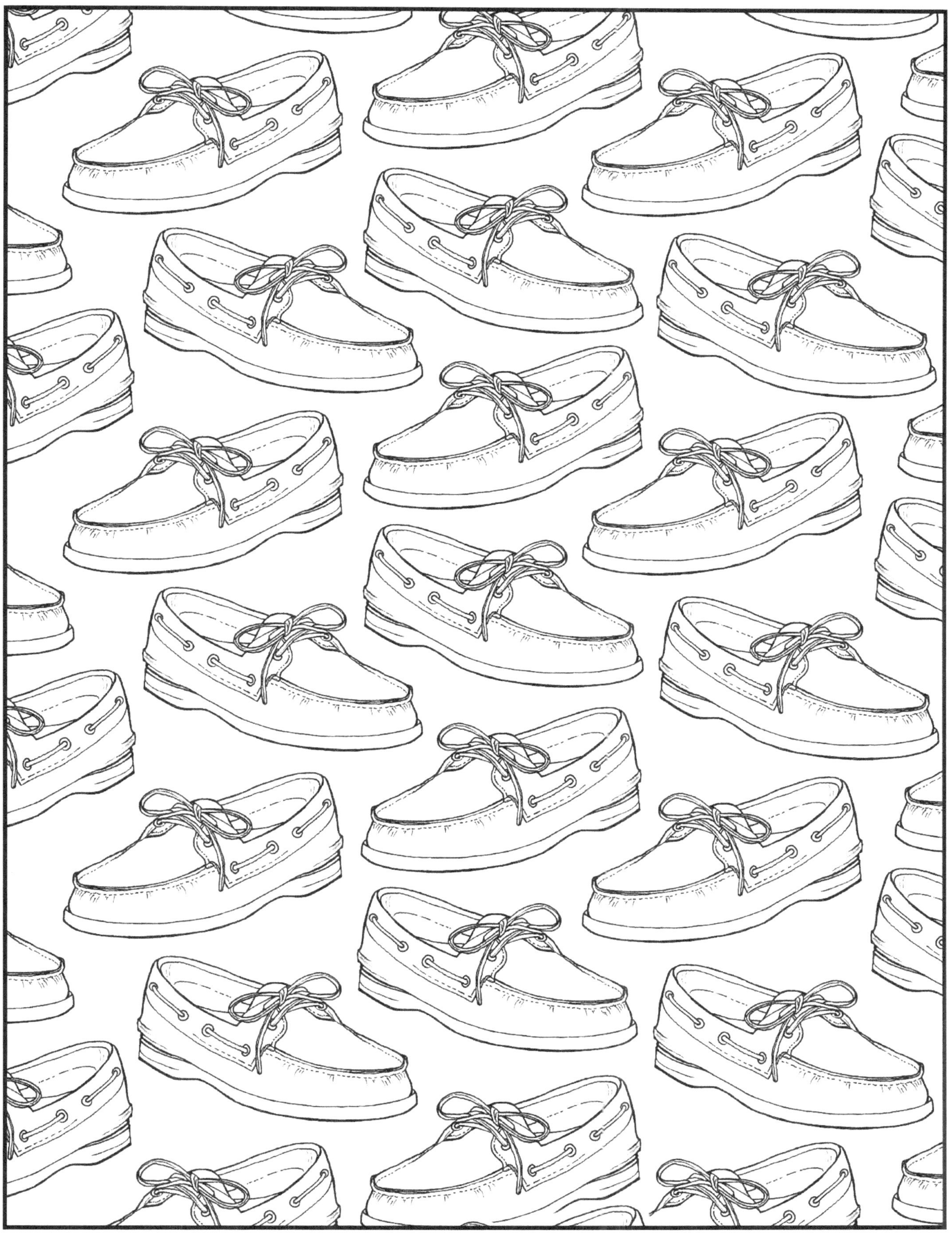

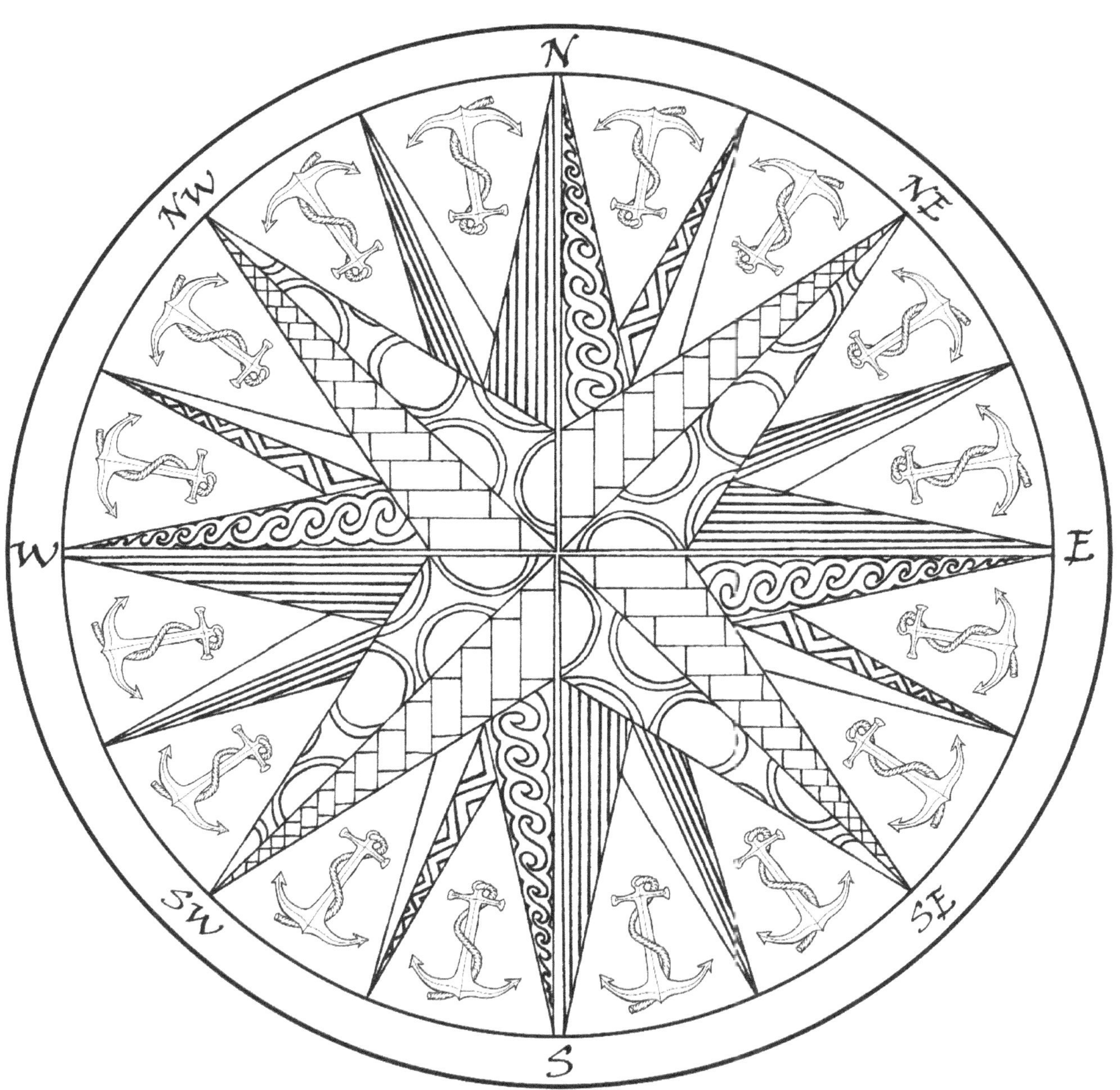

N
NW
NE
W
E
SW
SE
S

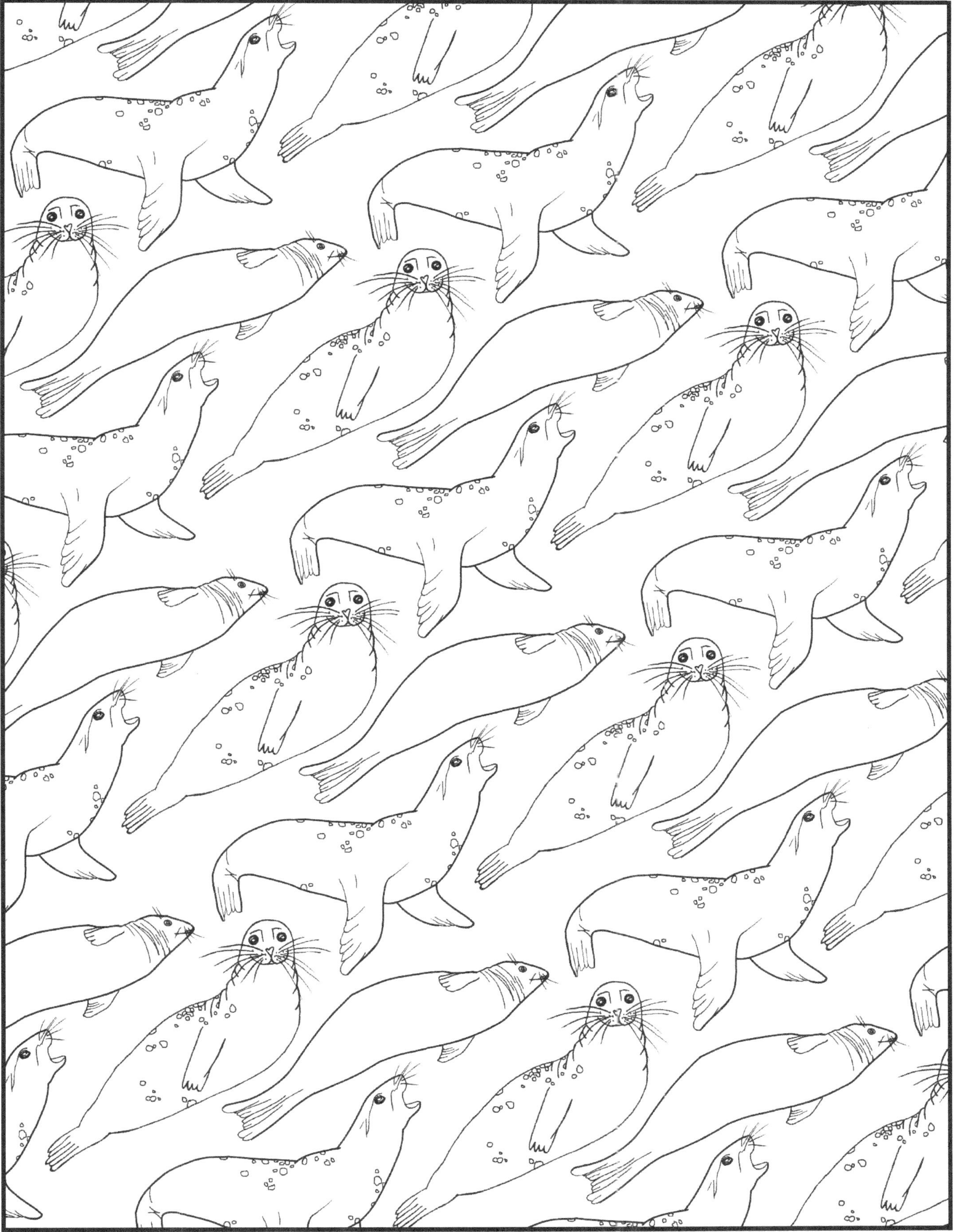

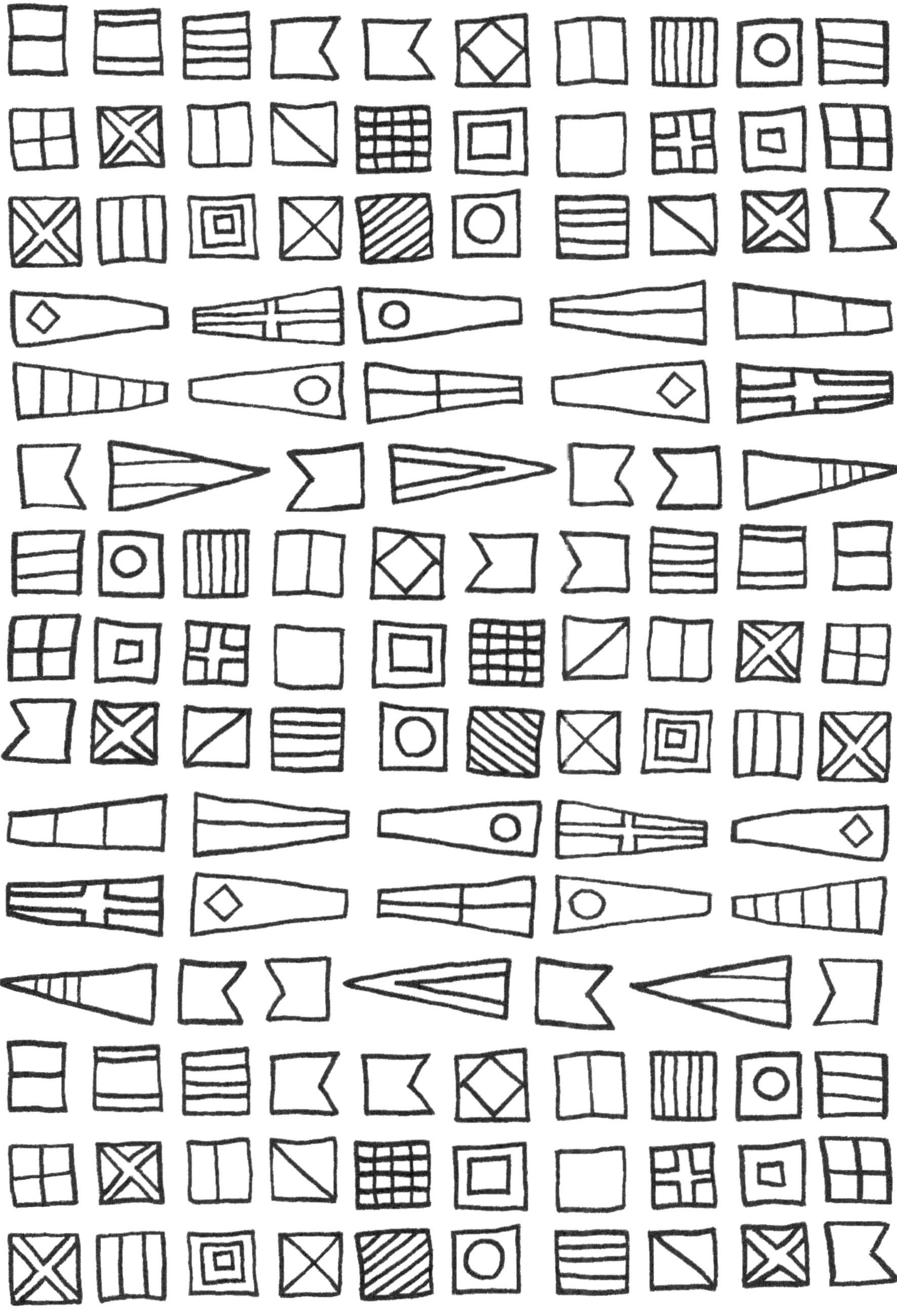

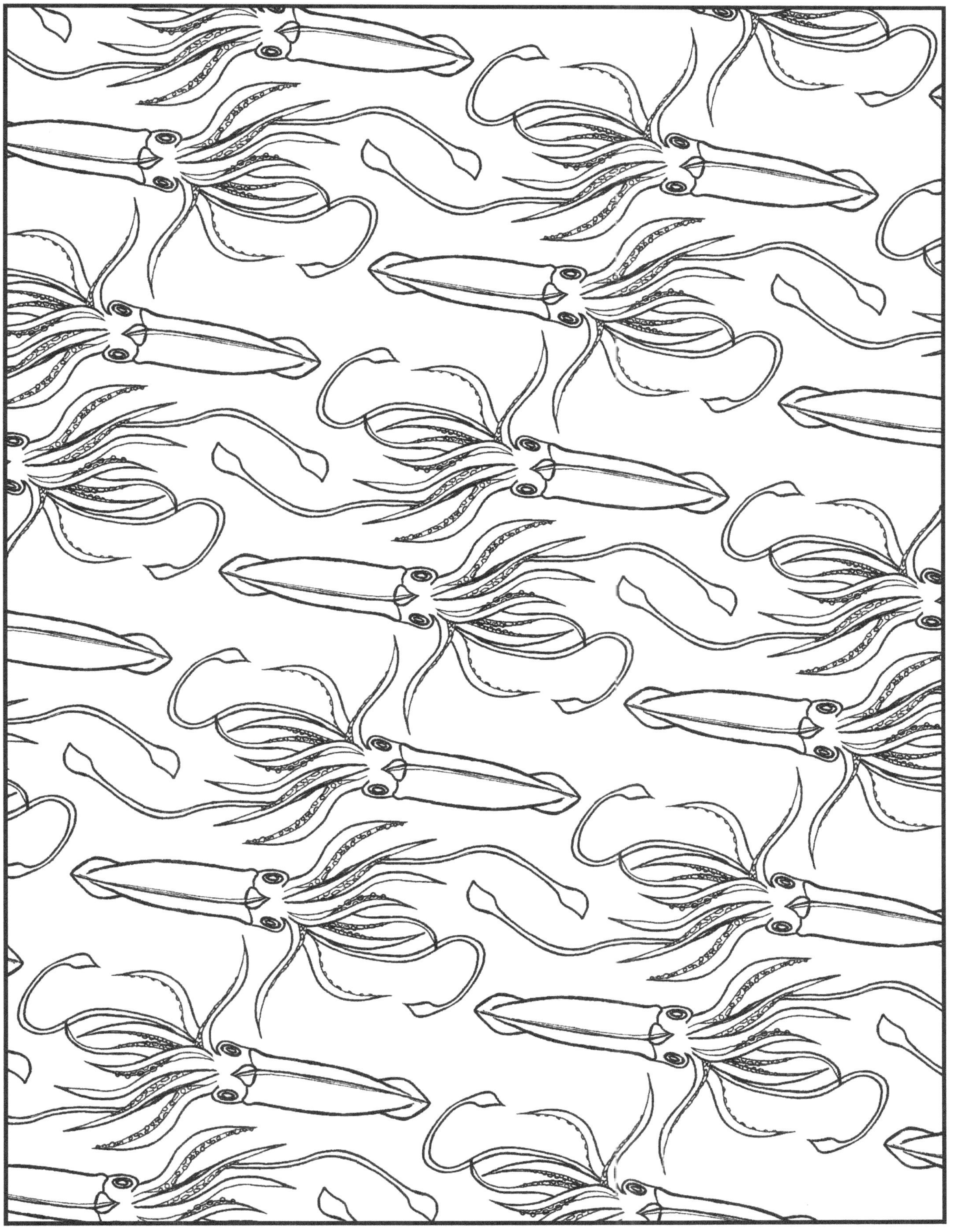

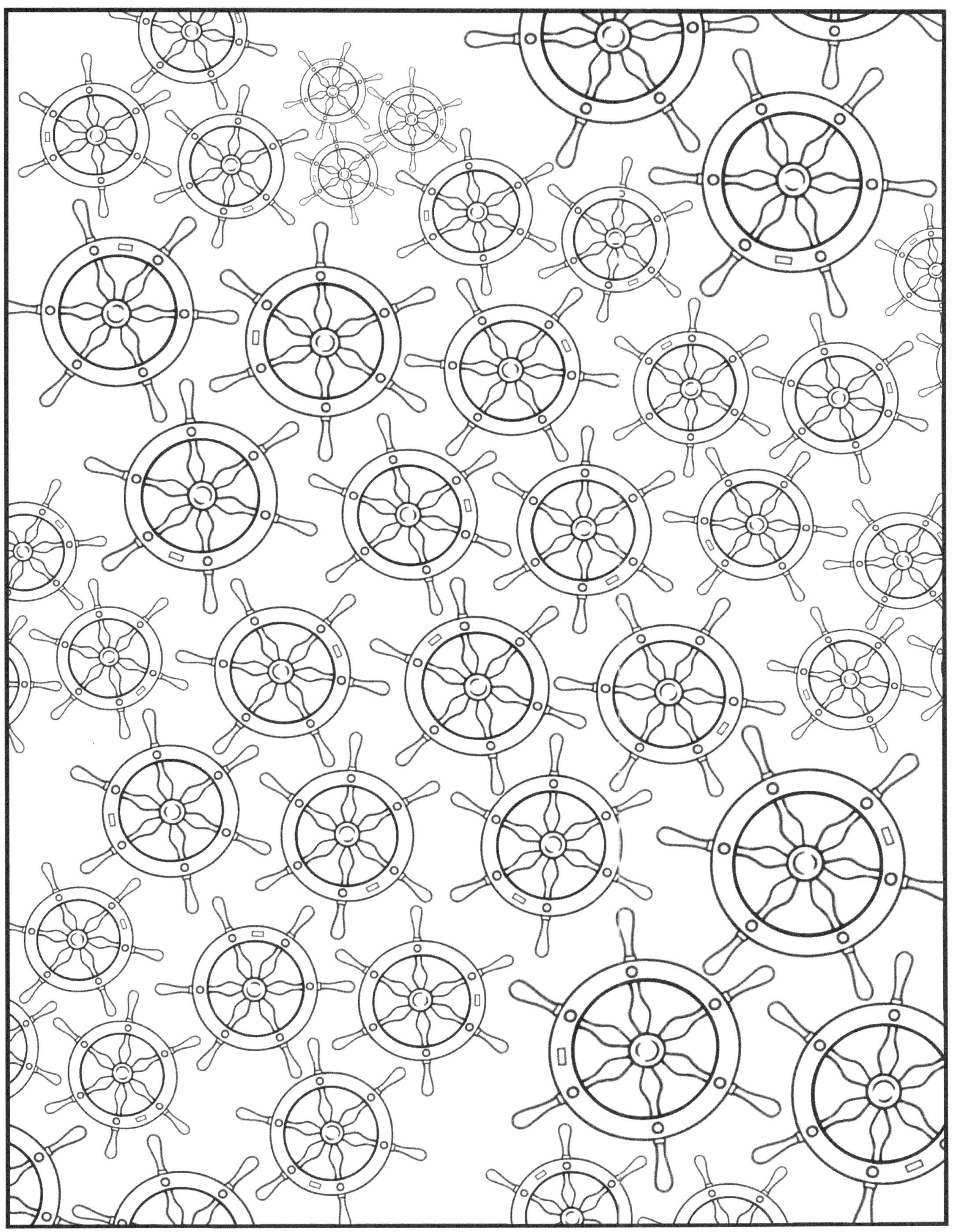

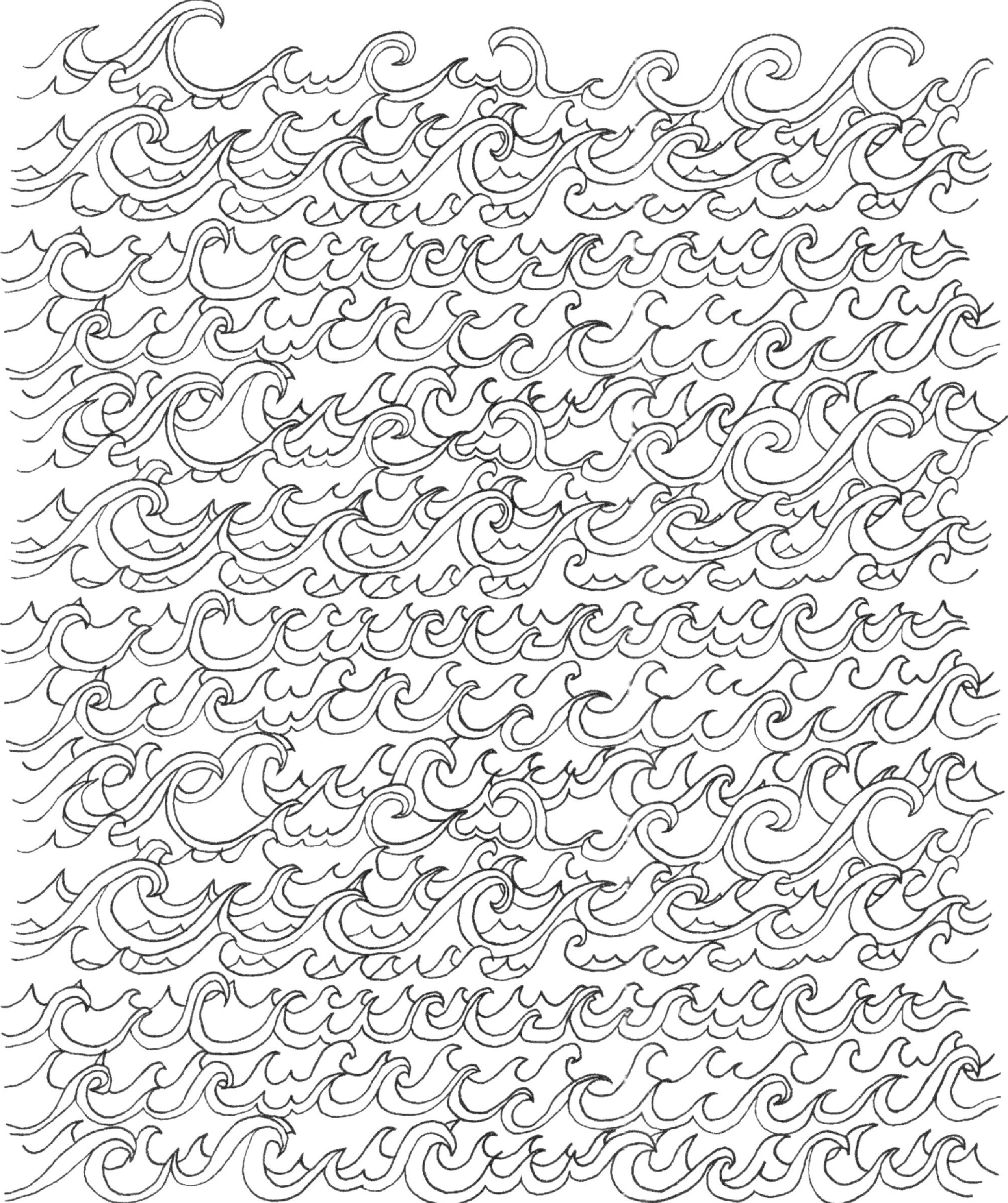

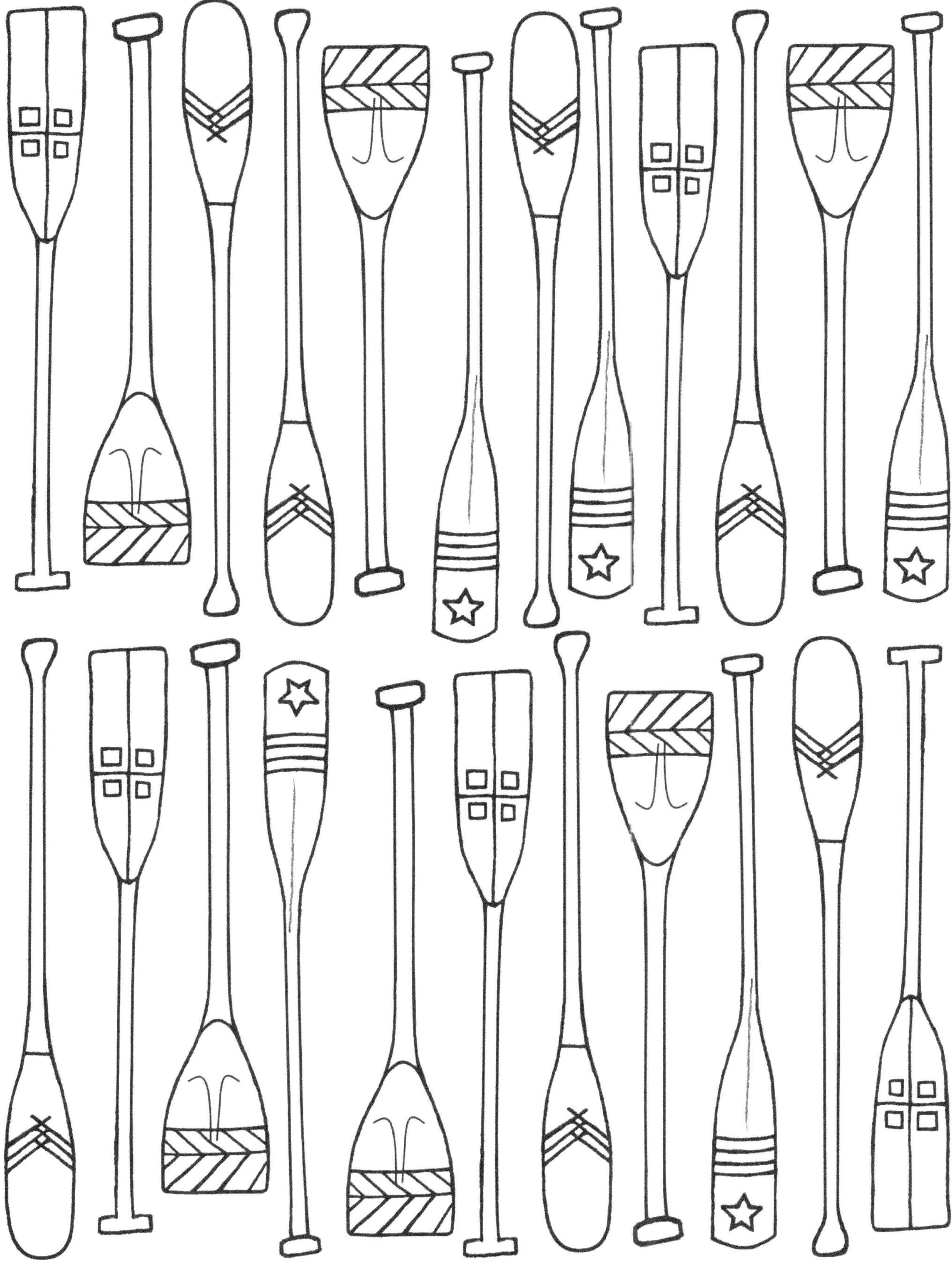

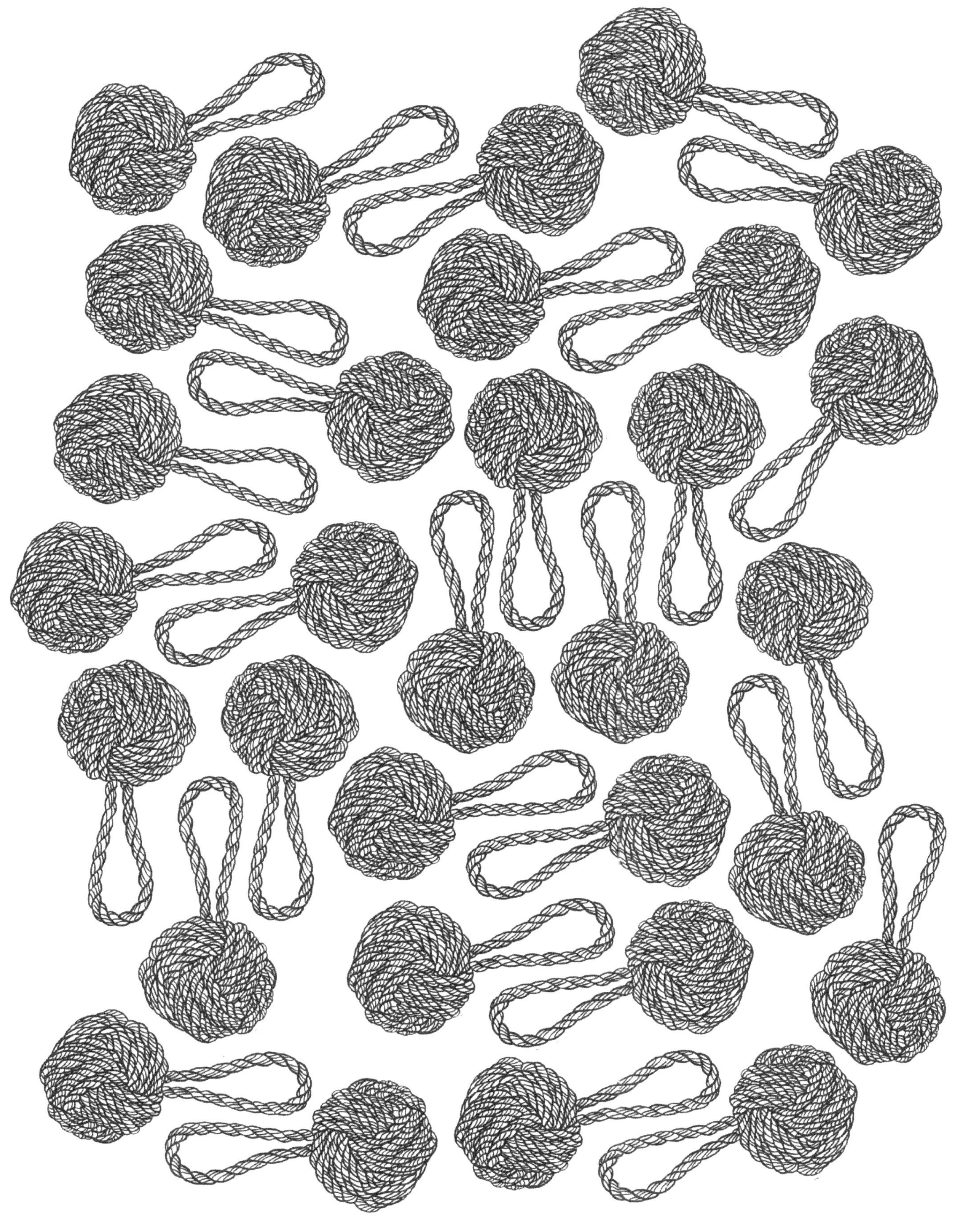

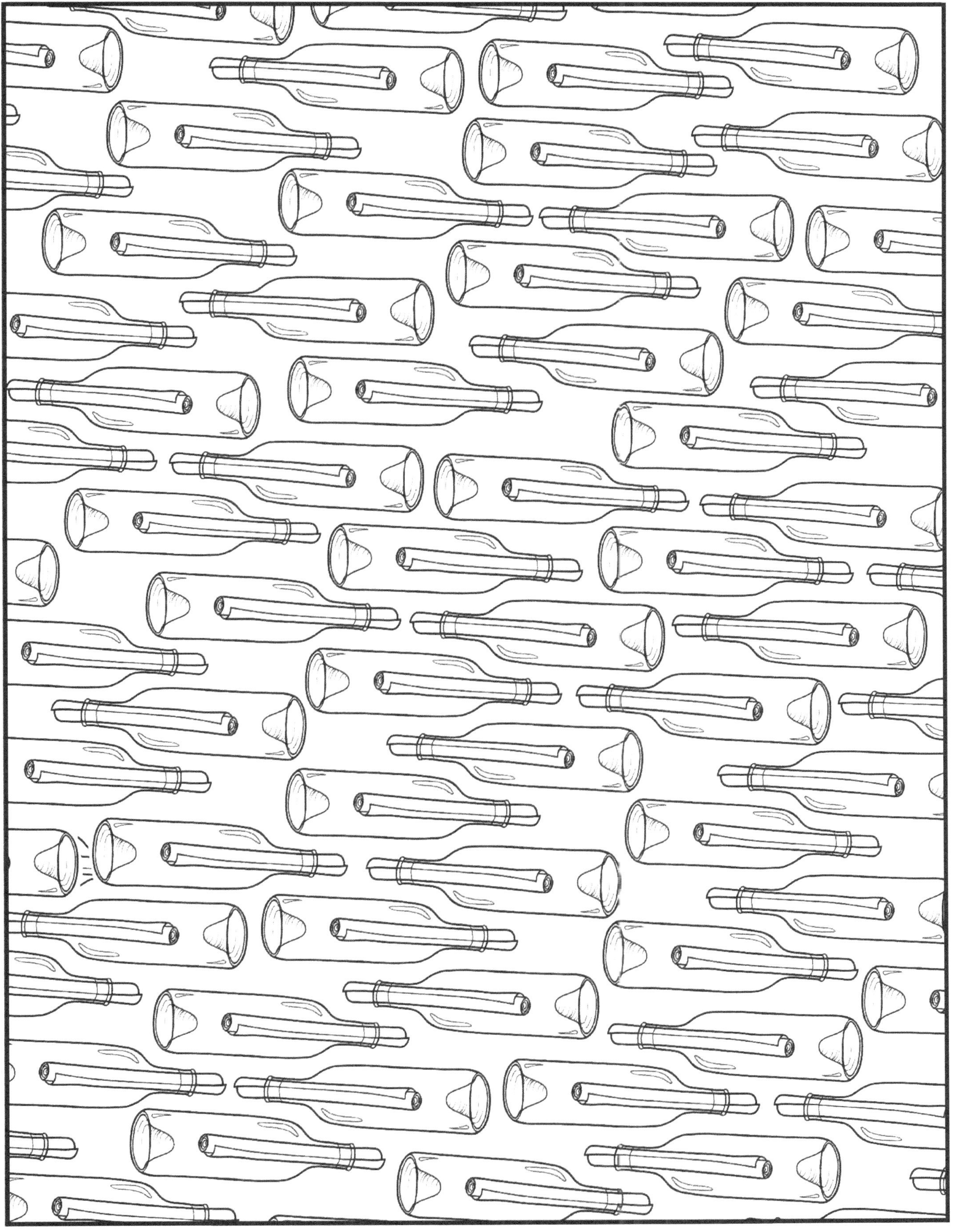

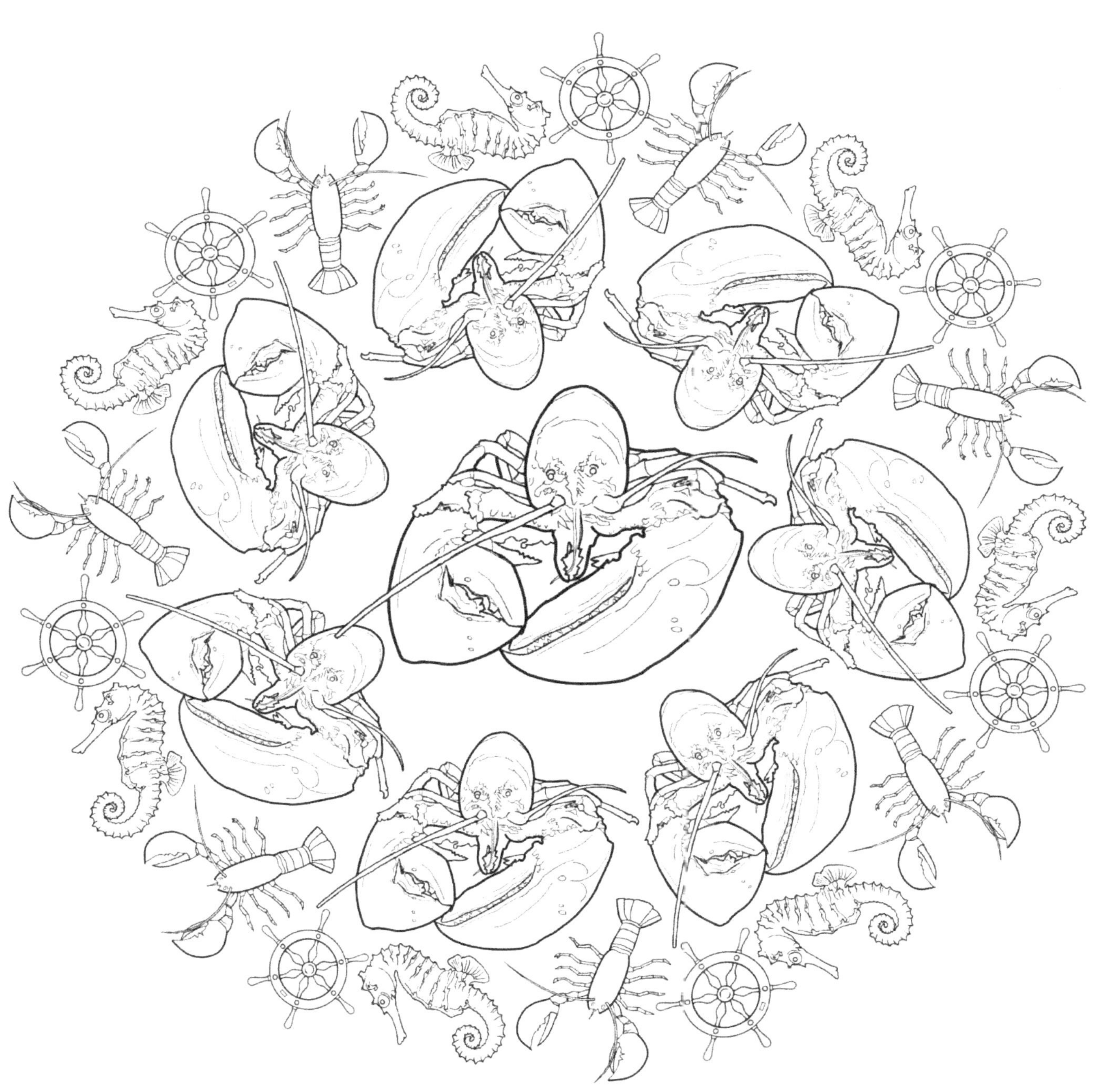

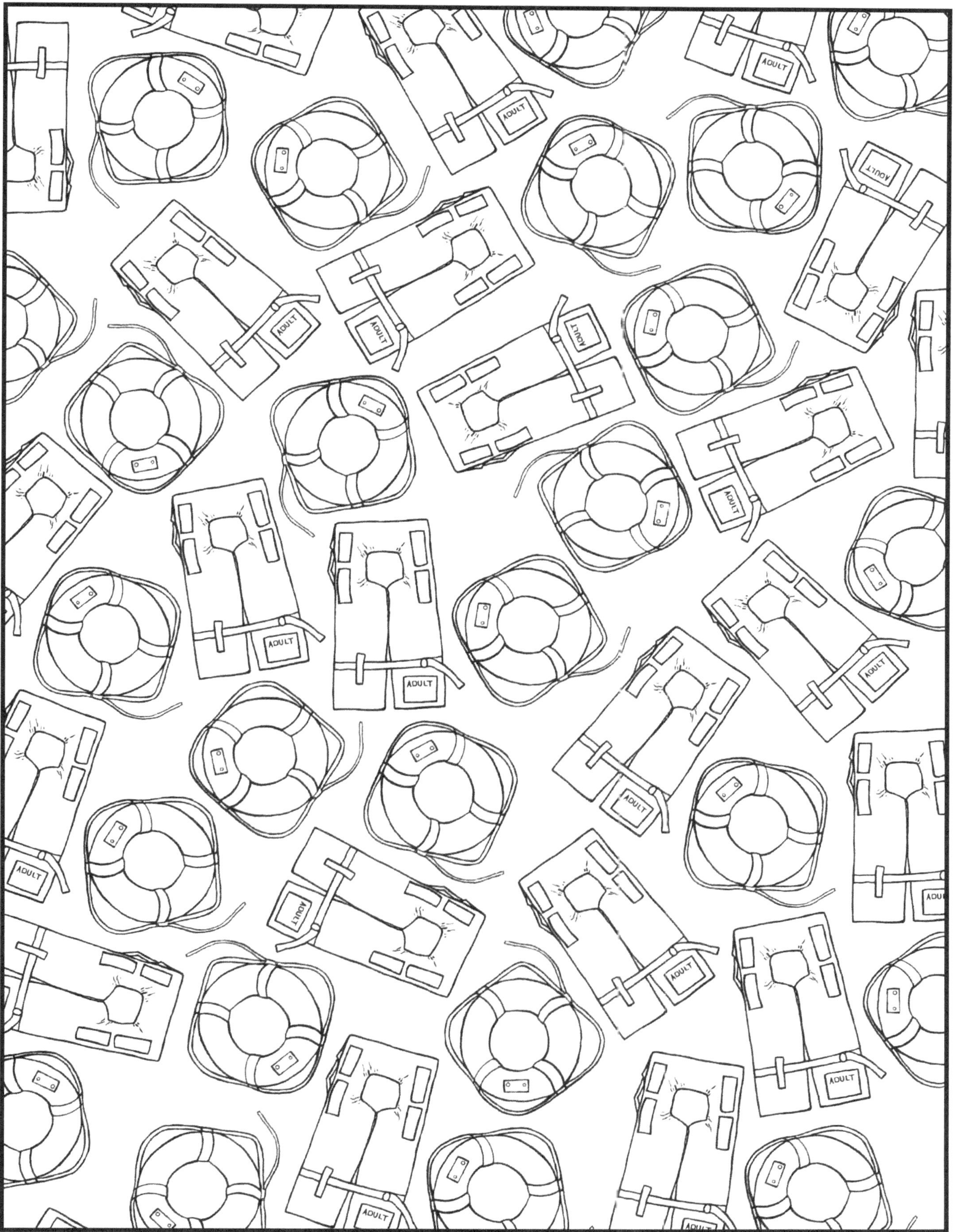

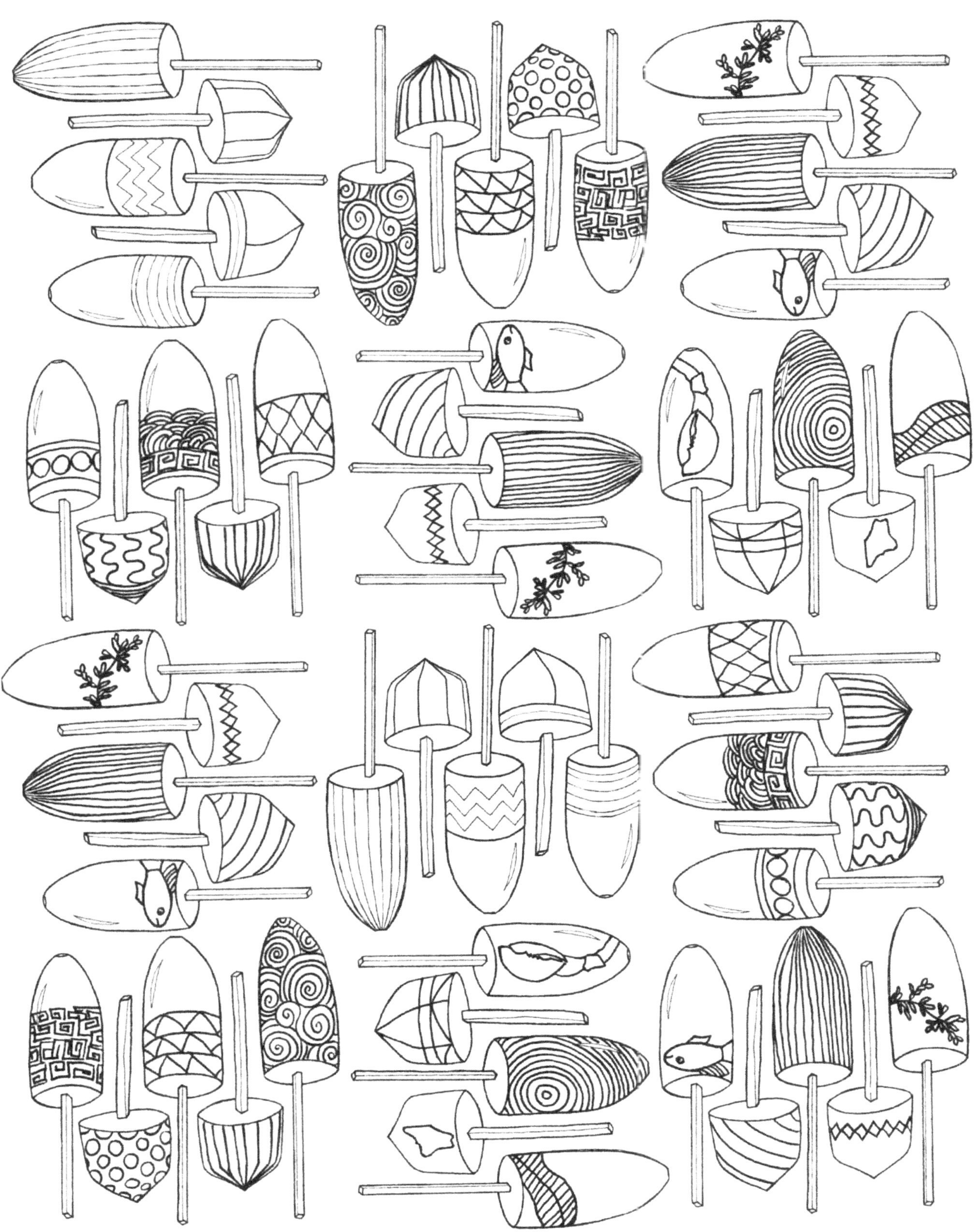

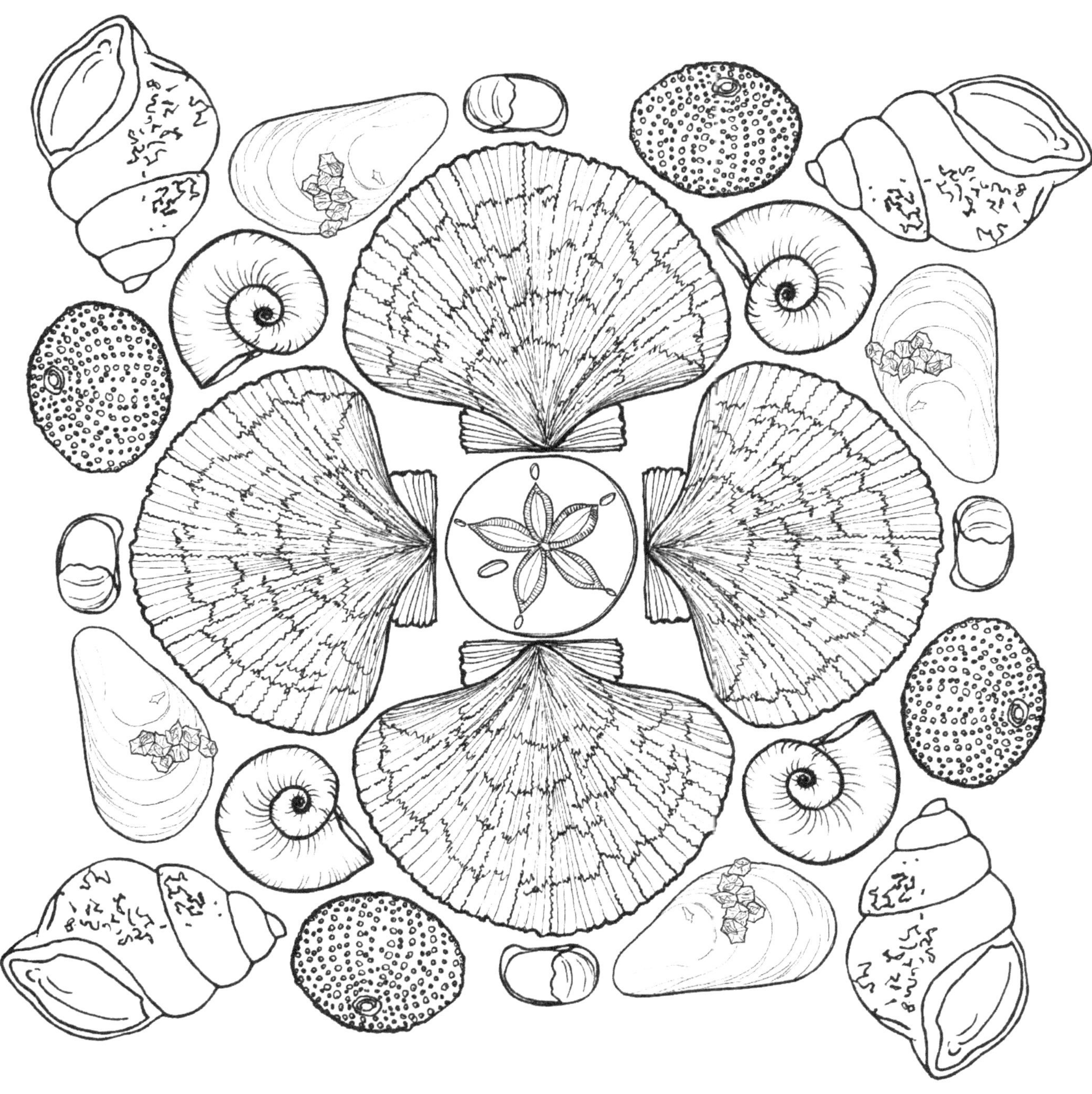

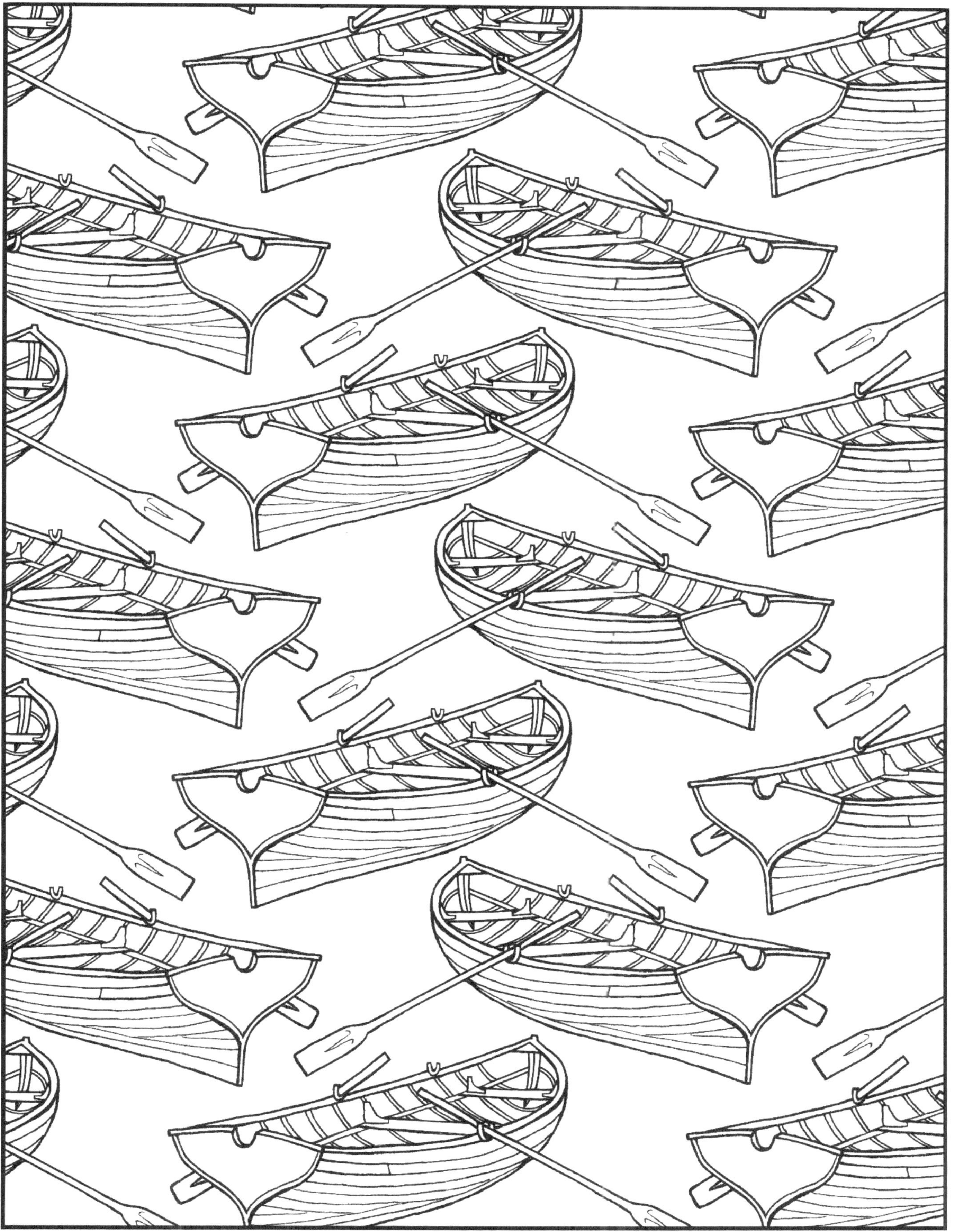

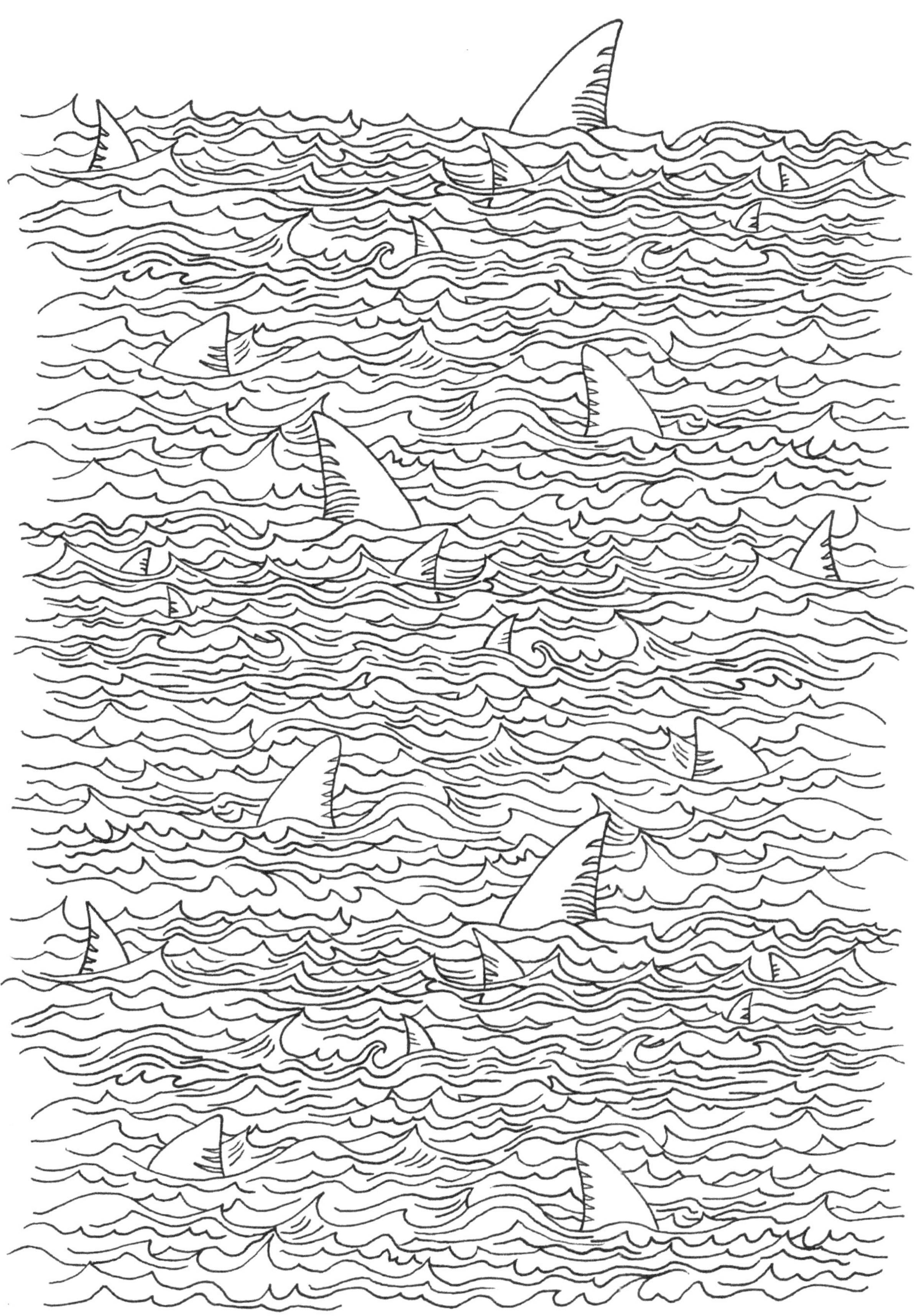

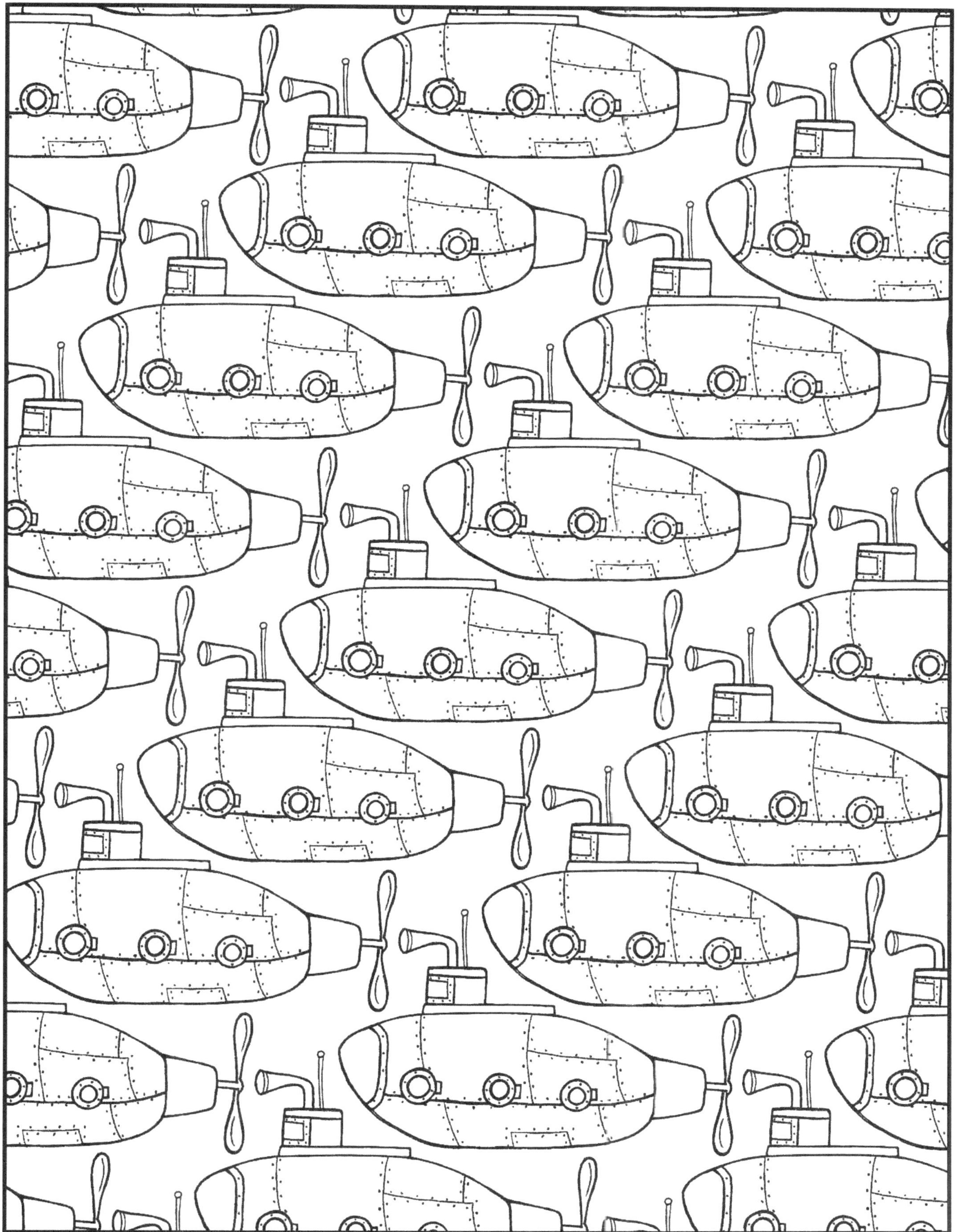

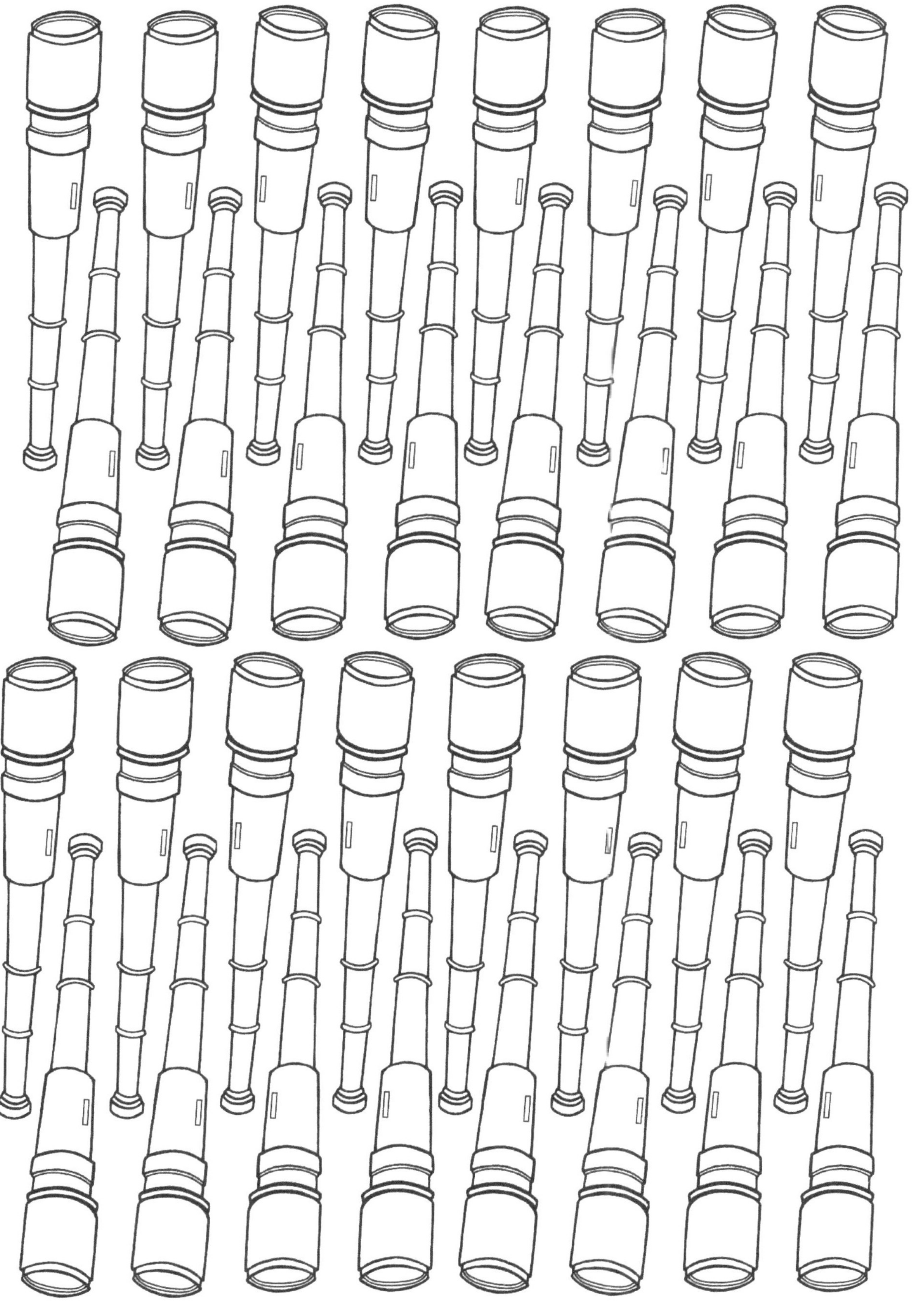

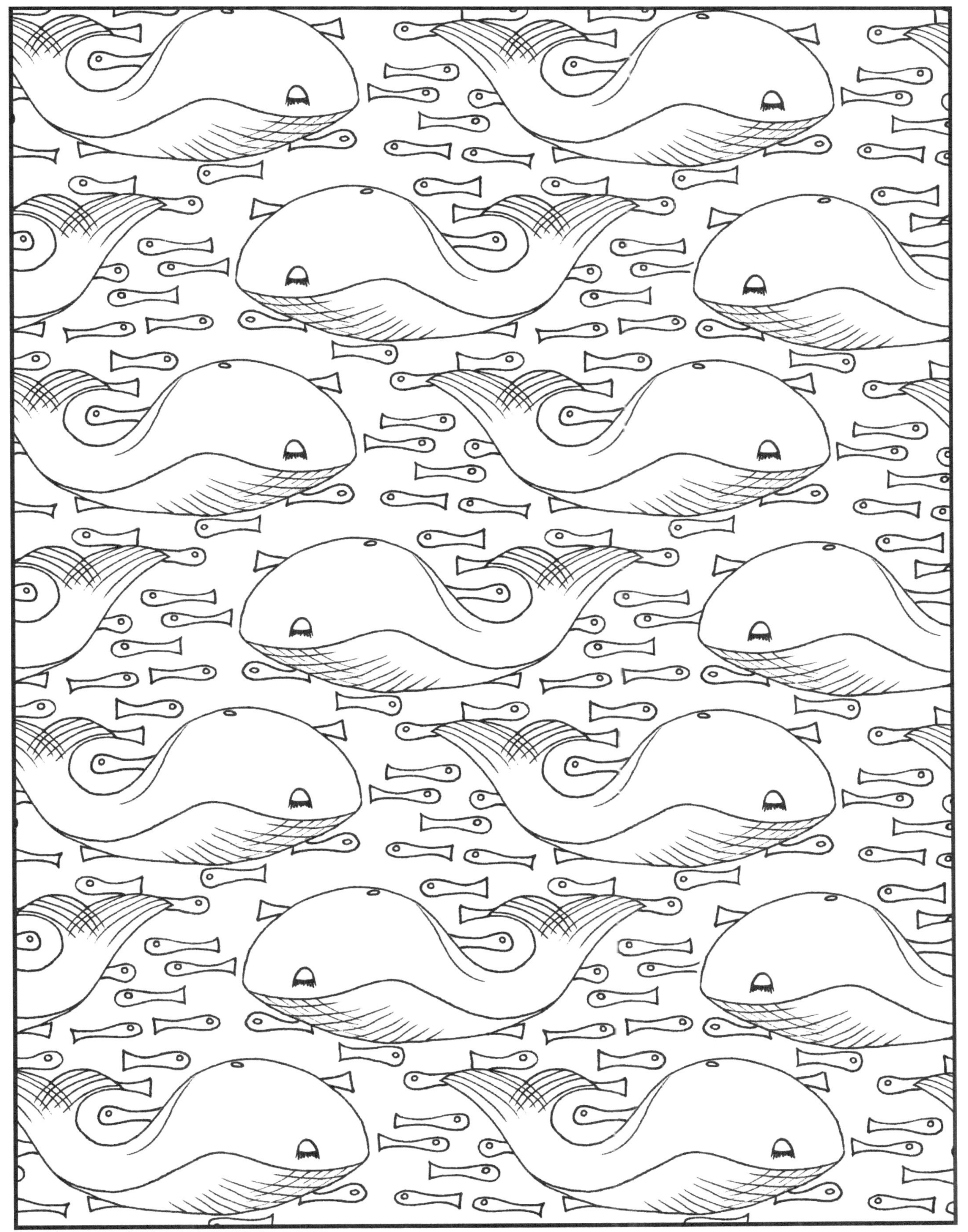

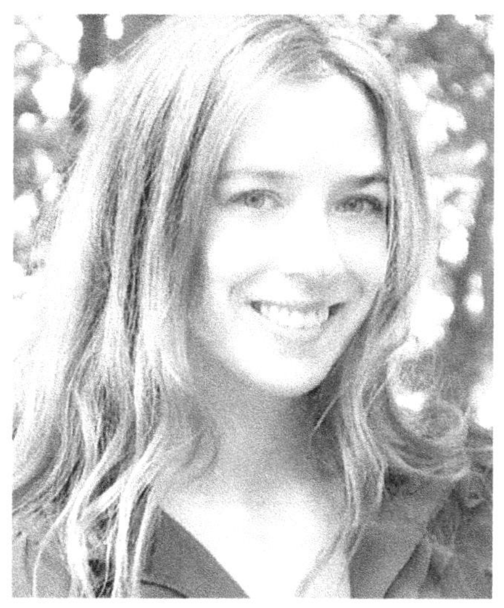

ABOUT THE ARTIST

Becky Chase was born and raised in Portland, Maine and grew up spending summers on an island in Casco Bay. She created *Nautical Namaste: A Sealife Pattern Escape* as a companion to her popular coloring book, *Downeast Daydream: A Maine Coloring Vacation.*

Though Becky has been creating art since childhood, her practice in line drawing began in 2011. To view more of her artwork, visit www.twinfawnmedia.com.